ME
mixed emotions

ME
mixed emotions

from the desk of

Andrew Nguyen
&
Pauleanna Reid

MERAKI HOUSE

P U B L I S H I N G

(C) 2018 by Pauleanna Reid

Published by
MERAKI HOUSE PUBLISHING INC.

For any information regarding permission contact
Pauleanna Reid via

pauleanna@pauleannareid.com

Printed in the United States of America
First publication, 2018.

Paperback ISBN 978-1-988364-30-8

DISCLAIMER

If you're reading this book, then you're trying to figure some things out, and we're glad to help. But before you dive in, we just want to offer one disclaimer: If you're looking for a magic formula or secret process that's going to guarantee you instant success, you've got the wrong book. (We're pretty sure that book doesn't exist at all.) What we share in these pages are our personal experiences, our hard-learned lessons, and the tips and advice that have helped us chase our dreams. We're not gurus or magicians, just two hard-working millennial entrepreneurs who want to see you win. So, we promise to give you the best of what we know. But the rest, that's up to you.

DEDICATION:

Pauleanna:

For my family. Every late night, last-minute flight, and crazy adventure along this journey is inspired by one goal: to make sure we'll have all the things we ever need to be happy.

Andrew:

Dedicated to everyone who actually reads this book.

HOW TO USE
THIS BOOK:

We met at a conference. Two people in a room bustling with "networkers" fighting to be seen and heard. We were on the perimeter, watching and listening. Not because we're shy. Have you met us? Not a shy bone in either one of our bodies. We weren't in the mix of it all because we knew what we were looking for: people who ate, slept, and breathed hustle. That's why we connected. We knew we both had what the other person wanted. Big ideas, bold vision, and a keen understanding of the power of collaboration. That first meeting was the tiny seed that grew into the book in your hands right now. Two like-minded millennial entrepreneurs on a mission to help people like you get closer to success. We've had countless conversations about our journeys, from our adventures in corporate to our wins in entrepreneurship. Between us, we have five successful businesses, more than a decade of experience, and hundreds of tips that we picked up along the way. And we've written it all down here. All the stories, lessons, challenges, failures, comebacks, and wins that got us to this point are in these pages.

It's a lot, we know. But we're not sorry about it. We wanted to give you as much as we could—all the things we wish we knew when we started. Now, it's all yours. So, settle in and get comfy.

Get out your highlighters, stickies, and bookmarks, and flip over to the table of contents. We've divided the book into three sections: "For People Who Don't Know What They Want," "For Corporate 9-5ers," and "For Entrepreneurs." You're free to read from beginning to end, jump in at the section that best suits where you are now, or skim through our headline tips and read the bits that catch your eye. It really doesn't matter. The choice is yours.

Whether you're an entrepreneur, a 9-5er, or somewhere in between, while you've got this book in your hands, you're the boss. Our advice is just that: advice. Take what suits you, your life, and your goals, and leave the rest.

We know first-hand that there is more than one way to entrepreneurial success — we have two totally different stories, and we don't agree on every single thing.

From time to time, we have opposing views throughout the book. We're not stressing about it, and neither should you. There might be times that you agree with one of us more than the other, or times when the best thing for you is somewhere in the middle of our perspectives. That's cool too.

All we want is for you to get the most out of this book for you and your journey.

- Pauleanna

INTRODUCTION:

The day I quit my corporate job in 2014 was the most amazing day of my life, I kid you not. I felt like I was born again. It felt like retiring. I felt the way you feel when you order ten chicken wings and end up getting eleven. (Shoutout to all my Instagram followers for that meme.) That was a huge step towards the life of my dreams, the life I have today that's full of excitement, enthusiasm, travels, and joy. For a while now, people have been asking me to write a book about my experiences. And over the past four years, I've been writing, but I've just been saving it in my notes because I was still waiting for the right moment.

You see, so many people have a desire to do something, but they make the biggest mistake by rushing. Doing things too early is not the wave. You might be saying "too early?" Because everybody preaches "start now!" and "it's never too early!" And that's true in certain situations, but not here. If I dropped a book right after quitting my job and before I built anything legitimate, sure a hundred of my friends might buy my book, but then what? I put in hundreds and hundreds of hours to sell a hundred books? No, when I do something I want the absolute best. I want it to have a multiplier effect. I want it to go viral. I want 1,000 comments and likes and shares. Don't you?

Now the time and the circumstances finally feel right. And I am so grateful to have made it to the point to write this book, and that you've picked it up. It's really crazy to me that I'm in such an amazing situation right now to not only provide for myself and my team, but to every single person who follows, reads, and engages with me and my brand. I do see it as a huge privilege to have any influence on people, whether it's 10 or 10,000. That gratitude has been one of the secrets of my success from the very beginning of my journey.

I'm not even going to hold back in this book; this is too important. I don't normally curse, so know that what I'm about to say right now is serious and I need you to get this next point through your f*ckin' skull, even if it's the only thing you get out of this book: Be grateful. Seriously, I challenge you right here and now to stop reading for 30 seconds and just breathe in the life that was given for your unique beautiful self. Then take the next 30 seconds and think of three things you're grateful for. The fact that you can read this book. Hell, the fact that you can read at all, that you have a roof over your head, that you have someone in your life that you can talk to (and if you don't have someone, shoot me an email or a DM right now, and I'll be that person for you). Do this every single morning for a week and see if your life doesn't change. Ladies and gentlemen, gratitude breeds confidence, confidence breeds clarity, clarity eliminates fear, and when you are no longer fearful, you can change the F*CKIN' WORLD.

That's where I want you to start with this book, with gratitude. Then I want you to add open-mindedness. Because Pauleanna and I are probably going to go against a lot of what you've been told your whole life. We'll contradict 90% of the stuff you hear on the internet. We know that there are a thousand coaches, gurus and internet marketers trying to sell you strategies. Everybody and their momma is an expert now, but a lot of the things they're pushing are plagiarized, stolen, and regurgitated, and half of them aren't nearly as successful as they pretend to be.

We want you to stop following that crowd, the people who haven't proven themselves. Stop following brands you don't know and the flashy things that have no substance. As the saying goes, you shouldn't be taking constructive criticism from people who've never constructed anything. Pauleanna and I practice what we preach, and we've used everything we've written here to build our empires. We're not here to trick you into anything. We lay it all out so you can decide for yourself that we're the real deal.

We want to cut through the BS and serve up proven strategies and genuine advice that comes from real, hard-earned experience. So, if you believe in what we do, who we are, and what we've created, then sit back and enjoy this book. (And if not, close the book or give it away. No hard feelings.)

If you stick with us, I hope that as you read these pages, you make it a conversation between myself, Pauleanna, and you, the reader. I challenge you to say "What if?" instead of "WTF?" when we say things that make you uncomfortable. Ask yourself, "What if these challenges are correct? What if this mindset is right? What if this perspective that I'm gaining could change my life?" You might be surprised by the answers. And if we can challenge at least one doubt you have, we've done our job for whatever investment you made that put this book in your hands.

We want this book to be the beginning of something bigger for you. We hope that it's going to offer you some ideas and inspiration for that "aha!" moment. It might begin with "I like this, and I like that, and I like this" (*cues 90's r&b song*). Then you slowly pick it up, until you're running around smiling with excitement because of your new discovery. You know what that good feeling is? Potential! And so, after every chapter of this book, I honestly hope that you feel a little bit closer to your potential, a little bit closer to realizing your dreams, and a little bit closer to satisfying your deepest desires.

Alright, here we go!

- *Andrew*

TABLE OF CONTENTS

FOR THOSE
WHO DON'T KNOW
WHAT THEY WANT

Chapter 1:
More than a Mess

Pauleanna

It's easy to think that successful people have no idea what it's like to feel like a mess, but believe me when I tell you that's far from the truth. I spent four terrible years in high school where I was badly bullied. I was the girl hiding out in the bathroom or library to get away from the drama that seemed to follow me everywhere. If you did see me, I was either killin' it on one of the sports teams or hanging with "friends" who weren't real friends at all. And then I went to college and ended up dropping out, suffering from depression, and trying desperately to figure out what to do with my life. I was 21, and I felt like an absolute mess.

All of that gave me a low opinion of myself. One of the biggest battles of my life was conquering the negative voices inside my head.

They told me things like:
"You are unworthy."
"You don't deserve to be here."
"Don't pursue your dreams."

As a result, I delayed and blocked my blessings. After acknowledging why this was happening, I had to strategize how to combat it. At the time, I'll be honest, I didn't know where to turn. At my lowest state of depression, when it seemed like my life was falling into a million pieces, I knew the one thing that could and would turn things around was my perspective. Before making any plans, I realized I had to shift my mindset. I had overdosed on motivational mixtapes, YouTube videos, and books. There's no lack of content online if you ever need a push in the right direction. But how do you pull away from watching endless amounts of Tony Robbins, Myles Monroe, and Joyce Meyers on the couch and start putting lessons into action?

You don't have to have all the answers. Just mix action with an ounce of purpose.

I started small by waking up daily with an agenda. And I don't just mean some days. I mean every single day. I was extremely calculated about where I directed my energy and how I used my time. Then I slowly started changing the language that once occupied an overwhelming portion of my mind.

"You are smart."
"You are beautiful."
"Your contribution matters."

Are you on top of the thoughts that are constantly on your mind?

Today, I still wake up to sticky notes with positive affirmations. These reminders are placed on nearly every piece of furniture around my bedroom, so I'm constantly surrounded by words that speak life into my next steps, even if I don't always understand what that bigger picture looks like.
Another tool that has helped me is writing.

Because you find yourself when you're by yourself.

My mind has always been full of ideas, dreams, and, just like you, things I worry about. I need somewhere to put it all. Writing in a journal has always been a big part of my life. This practice helped me define my next steps at a time when I was feeling very lost. Writer's block didn't exist because I had so many questions about life that I was trying to solve and, believe it or not, the most enjoyable part of this process is trying to figure it out.

I love how freeing writing is. It doesn't have to be perfect. It doesn't have to be about anything in particular. Most mornings, I wake up early and freewrite for ten minutes. I have notebooks with drawings, scribbles, notes to self, and my innermost thoughts. Sometimes, those thoughts lead me to another thought that leads me to a partial answer I'm looking for. Unorganized thoughts are the best. There are times when I look down at my paper and don't know what the heck I've just scribbled or wrote, but then, as soon as I need it, the words or pictures jump off the page. Over time, more "aha!" moments occurred, and I really started to see what I wanted for myself.

Experimentation, journaling, and mind-shifting are great, but at some point, you have to decide what you want.

Clarity comes from obsession.
Get obsessed.

To climb out of the hole I was in meant it was time to narrow my focus and limit all distractions. There was no degree to fall back on, I didn't have rich parents, and I definitely didn't have a baller boyfriend either. Taking a risk meant honoring my feelings and knowing that somehow, I'd figure this shit out. It took a while before I found my rhythm. But I did, gradually. Each day, I took a step forward and celebrated small victories to help maintain my confidence and self-esteem.

As the "aha!" moments kept coming, I took things a step further by transitioning my newfound inspiration onto a vision board. (I made my first board in college.) I'm a visual learner, which means I think in pictures. Journaling may have opened the gateway to my dreams, but once I started creating vision boards, I dreamed in full color. And then to get things off the vision board and happening in real life, I used this dope eight-step goal setting process that might help you get going too.

1. Write all your goals down. Yes, all of them. Then order them by priority. Put the goal that matters most right now at the top of the list. Why? Because it will help you operate with a sense of urgency. And urgency gets shit done.

2. Weigh the pros and cons of your goals. Seeing the positives will inspire you and knowing the consequences will help you prepare for the challenges to come.
3. Kill those limiting beliefs that are in the way. I'm serious. Shut them down. Remember, mindset is everything. There's no room for excuses, low standards, procrastination, or any of that. Find new, productive ways of thinking to help you get where you want to be.
4. Hit the books. Seek out the educational resources that will help you speed up the process of achieving your goal. And while books and podcasts are great, nothing beats real life experience, even if that means you have to travel, intern, volunteer, or hire a consultant who already knows the ropes.
5. Find your role models. Chances are there's someone out there who's an expert at the thing you want to do, or at least doing something very similar. Get obsessed with them and use them as a guide. But be wary. Not everybody who looks like they have it all really does, so don't get sidetracked by shitty advice and highlight reels.
6. Get accountable. Whether it's in an online forum, Facebook group, or your circle of friends, find people who will hold you accountable to your goals, especially for things you've quit on before.
7. See the bigger picture. Every goal you achieve sets you up for something else. So, always consider how your goal is preparing you for the other things you want in your life. I'll give you an example. It's a big goal for me to work directly with Shonda Rhimes. Writing for Forbes? A big step in the right direction. And about a hundred other little goals helped me land that Forbes gig. Every step counts.
8. Recognize how your goals will shape you. Everything you do as you work towards your goals, and the way your life changes when you achieve them, is going to change who you are as a person. Make sure it's for the better.

Stop worrying about big goals and ideas. Build brick by brick.

At first, my goals were really simple. A good portion of my vision board collage represented the person I wanted to become - strong, intelligent, career-savvy, and happy. As a result of searching for these things (that were already inside of me though I didn't know it), the journey encouraged me to think bigger and my goals transitioned into tasks like developing better time management skills, learning to socialize, not crumble in crowded spaces, build positive friendships, set aside time for self-care, and find more ways to be independent—or figure out what that even means to me.

Inspiration hit when these small goals were achieved. Not immediately, but over the course of several months to a year, I was in a position to stand up for myself, advocate for myself, and ask more of myself. The first major goal that I wanted more than anything was to find a mentor. From studying successful people over the years, I realized two things: every great artist was once an amateur, and to be great, at some point in their career, they had to stand on the shoulders of a mentor.

A good mentor will help you filter through all the info and advice to custom tailor a path for you.

One strategy that made a huge difference was becoming more observant of the people around me. Yes, I wanted mentors who were present in my day-to-day life, but that didn't stop me from finding online mentors. Too many to name, too many to choose from. To keep from being overwhelmed, I developed a habit of studying two CEOs every month. I studied everything about these individuals, from their morning routines to people management skills, from their top strengths to how they handle and defuse a crisis in their company.

I studied their habits and qualities. I read every social post and article, watched every video interview, added them on LinkedIn, and even went so far as reaching out and saying hello or offering to take something off their plate. That's how I met founders Rakia Reynolds of Skai Blue Media and Bea Arthur of The Difference in 2013. And recently, I've had the chance to sit down with founders Jason Saltzman of Alley and Jason Field of Brainstation. This all took time. Through it all, I aggressively took notes while being very patient with the process. This career recipe laid a solid foundation for what is now my success story.

I want to stay on the subject of mentorship for a second. It's something I can't stress enough and a piece of advice that you'll hear me say a lot throughout this book. You need to get a mentor. It's so important that you surround yourself with people who can help you win.

Build your personal board of advisors, your winners circle.

You'll hear a lot of gurus tell you that you shouldn't ask anyone to be your mentor right off the bat, that you should build organically. While it is very true, and they aren't wrong, I have to admit that I met my first mentor in 2010 (I was 22 years old at the time) and approached a bit differently.

Shannae Ingleton was my first ever mentor. At the time, she was the founder of a company called What Women Want. While scrolling my Facebook timeline, I discovered her and almost instantly started obsessing over her style and how she carried herself. It was effortless. I was equally impressed to know that she was a business owner, something I was still aspiring to at the time. An avid reader of her blog, I loved her ambition and secretly wanted to be her friend. I was in my early 20s and curious. I was still in the process of finding myself, and something in me said, 'Just ask her.' So, I did. I sent her a Facebook message and extended a dinner invitation. I remember it like it was yesterday. We went to Richtree on Yonge and Wellington in the heart of downtown Toronto. During our meetup, I learned more about her story and asked as many questions as I could. I'm grateful for Shannae because she gave me a chance. She replied 'yes' to a girl who had nothing and still invested in my future. She gave her time which evolved into a great friendship, and there are so many special moments that followed.

Shannae is the reason for my love for blogging. When we met, I was writing in a beat-up notebook, but she encouraged me to aim higher and start a blog on a platform called Blogspot. So, I did and used my new blog as an online diary. As our mentorship grew over time, so did Shannae's investment. After one year of blogging consistently, I receive a phone call that changed the course of my life forever. Shannae was on the other line and said, 'Hey, P! I have an opportunity for you that I think you'll be great at.' It was that phone call that led to an interview at one of Canada's most respected publishing houses. I went from blogger to nationally-published journalist just after my 23rd birthday. For the next four years, I was writing about world issues and politics, fashion and lifestyle, technology and environmental issues, as well as my favorite, celebrity inspiration stories with Olivia Newton-John, Rick Mercer, Dr. Mehmet Oz and his wife Lisa, and Jillian Michaels, just to name a few. My stories would garner an audience of several hundred thousand people across the country in various major newspapers.

This is such a huge lesson I will never forget. Produce quality work. Always. You just never know who is watching and what power they hold. Shannae had noticed my work ethic and the passion I had for my blog. I was also a guest contributor to her platform.

When she felt I was ready, she opened another door for me.

Hashtag. Blessed. Shannae and I have gone on to celebrate everything from birthdays to company launches, and career transitions to her wedding and the birth of her first child. The best career move I ever made was to advocate for myself and ask for help from people who wanted to see me win.

The day I realized I could be anything and everything I wanted to be is the day I chose to be great. But it took someone showing me that possibility. Now that I see much clearer, I know that God has bigger plans for my life that don't involve feeling sorry for myself or believing that I am broken.

So, honor your feelings, and if you are unsure how you feel, embrace that uncertainty. You owe it to you to see this process through. It's often the scariest choices that end up being the most worthwhile.

Andrew

A positive outlook is a major key for me. In fact, I would say keeping my mindset right is one of the top ten reasons my resume looks the way it does right now. I was fortunate enough not to have to battle mental illness, but the stress and struggle were still very real. Before I was running multiple six-figure businesses, building super cool brands, and touring across the country for speaking gigs, I was just a young, naive kid raised by immigrant parents who had nothing but vision and ambition to pass on to me. There was no money, no privilege, no silver spoon. At 18, I started at Hampton University with $80 in my bank account.

And that was just one of many low points for me. Trust me when I tell you I've been through it. School wasn't a breeze at all. I flunked out of some of my classes, lost scholarships, and got suspended. My bank account wasn't always stacked. I slept in my car when I didn't have rent money. I worked multiple jobs just to make ends meet. I even had to join the Marines and ship off to boot camp when I wanted to pursue my goals and dreams. Now, I'm not a big muscular dude. There's nothing fun about boot camp for a guy like me, but I had to make it work. Even when I started to see success in my business, there were struggles — the business deals that went south, the partners who screwed me over, the lawsuits I faced, and the ones I had to file, the thousands of dollars lost.

None of that was easy. And I'm not saying I went through any of it with a smile on my face. Sometimes, it really felt like I was going through more than my share. But one thing I learned over the past ten years of my life is that how you react to situations changes everything. When the punches are rolling in, if you can keep your mind right, hit back with positivity, and find a way to flip those situations to your advantage, you still win.

I have three tips that helped me keep pushing when my life felt like a mess.

Emotions are just a temporary way to respond to mess. Don't let them run things long-term.

Emotion, to me, is one of the most interesting human traits. From baby-like peacefulness to monstrous rage, they're inescapable and impact every part of our lives. When hard times come, when you fail, when life seems to be kicking your butt, it's easy for emotions like anger, sadness, and self-pity to kick in. But I've never found those to be productive. When I get angry, I don't think straight. When I let sadness take hold for too long, I lose the will to keep pushing. And self-pity has never changed a thing. I'm not saying I don't feel negative emotions. I'm human, just like you. But I just don't let them take up space in my head for too long. I talk a lot about pivoting, but it's not just for business tactics. I'm quick to pivot on my emotions too, and learning to master my them has helped me to master my life.

Fail fast, fail forward, fail until you can't fail anymore.

I've failed so many times it's not even funny. I've failed way more than I've succeeded. But I always say, fail fast and fail forward. Honestly, after you fail so many times, you learn what not to do. It's like playing a video game. It might take you 99 times to pass level four, but once you do, it's a thrill. Every time something went wrong – every time a business partner screwed me over, a deal went sour, a job opportunity fell apart – I figured out what I could make from the leftover pieces. A lot of people dismiss the idea of silver linings, but I really believe that if you want to, you can find something good out of even the worst situations, and that's how you win. I know how to look for opportunities, how to market, how to create value, grow a business, sign top-notch deals, how to read people, who to trust, and how to spot a scam. And I learned all of that because when life threw me challenges, I found a way to bounce back better than before. That's the thing. There are lessons in everything if you're looking for them. It's all about re-calibrating your mind towards seeing the good.

Gather clues left by others. Don't copy, take data points and form your own life's algorithm.

Richard Branson. Elon Musk. Gary Vee. Mark Cuban. All people I admire a lot. Not just because they've built million-dollar businesses, but because I love the way their minds work. How they think about things, how they solve problems, how they approach business and life in general. It's all amazing to me. The more I read their books, listen to their interviews, and watch their moves, the more I learn to think and operate like a winner, just like they do. What you feed your mind absolutely affects your mindset, so I'm always careful to fill up on positive influences.

I'm not saying any of this is foolproof, and it's definitely not easy. Sometimes, the struggle is going to be so real that positivity is going to seem impossible. But learning to keep a positive mindset is like learning to develop any skill. It takes practice. It takes standing back up every time struggle and failure knock you down and figuring out how to get better and do better.

If you're in a space in your life where you feel like everyone is passing you by, and you don't have a clue how to get your life together, I want to help you turn that around. Right here, right now, as you're reading this page, start looking at yourself and your life differently. Perspective is everything. If you think life sucks, go travel the world. If you can't travel, YouTube it and see how hard life really is for other people. Gratitude and appreciation will change your current life. Perspective will change your future output. Stop beating yourself up for all the times you failed, fell down, or got lost. Look back at your life and all the things you labeled a mess and start searching for those little gems and lessons. They're in there.

BEAT THE BULLY BLUES

Pauleanna

It's hard enough dealing with your own negative thoughts. Don't give other people space to add to that.

Stop explaining yourself to people who have already made up their minds about you.

It's super easy to feel crippled by opinions, stares and negative comments. It's even easier to fall into the trap and believe them. But a wise friend once told me that it's important to know you're important. Know your worth and add taxes.

I'll never forget the names of the people who have been the most critical in my life. The easiest and most immediate reaction is to despise them. But looking back I could say they were probably the most important people to me. The high school bullies who called me names I won't repeat, the teachers who failed me and called out my insecurities in class, and the family members who still don't know or understand what I do.

I don't think it's right. But personally speaking, it sparked something in me that I don't think I would have developed otherwise.

I know most advice tells us to avoid negativity, fall back from toxic friendships, block out the noise - which is true. However, on the other hand, I think a certain level of criticism is necessary. Had my parents not questioned my choices, I don't know if I would've ever learned to stand up for what I believed in. Had my friends never dissed me, I don't know if I would've ever got a damn backbone. Listen, dark times teach you a lot, and one of the greatest lessons I've come to realize is that there is life after disappointment. It's not the load that breaks you it's the way you carry it.

Once you distance yourself from negative people, you may not find positive ones right away. Mentors are not sitting on every corner just waiting for you to arrive. They are hustling, and they are busy. But I've always believed that if you want to do something badly enough you will teach yourself, and that's exactly what I did.

Hustle while you wait.

I continued writing and reading. I didn't always know if the next step was the right step, but I knew it was better than standing still. Even on the days I didn't want to do it, I talked myself into it. Procrastination is poison. My biggest fear was to be in the same place the following year. The question I ask myself every day before I jump out of bed is, 'Right now, in this very moment, what do I want the most?' Ask yourself the same, and whatever the answer is, give yourself permission to do it. We are so used to playing it safe that the moment something feels uncomfortable, we decline and dismiss. Through trial and error, I've learned how important it is to listen to your body. For some, it's the heart, and you'll know because it's beating so fast that you can barely breathe. Or perhaps you begin to break into a cold sweat—that's a sign, and it means something significant. Other people may experience a gut feeling and intuition steering them in a direction that makes no immediate sense—that's a sign, and it means something significant. Then there's your stomach which houses all your butterflies and creates a nervous feeling every time you do something that is outside your normal routine—that means something significant too.

Not knowing the answer is actually the best part.

I used to think whenever I felt extremely uncomfortable it was an alert; that my body was setting off the alarms and throwing up red flags. Sometimes, this is the case, but not as often as we think. I quickly discovered that the more I ran away from the issue or circumstance, the further away I was from actually resolving it. So, I started taking baby steps towards making discomfort my new normal. Personal growth is hard. It always feels uncomfortable at first, but soon you'll learn that the more you invest in yourself, the more control you have over your life – and I wanted control.

If you are feeling stuck but don't do anything about it, the outcome is 100% your fault. To get rid of this feeling and experience results you've never had, you're going to have to do some things you've never done before.

But I would've never been able to gain the courage to do anything outlined in this book had I not put this mindset into practice. And by practice, I mean, try new things on a small scale first. Like sign up for a new class, go to the movies alone, have coffee with an old friend, smile at a stranger, strike up a conversation with someone in line behind me. Start small. Think big.

Stop depending on other people. Find yourself and let everyone else be the cherry on top.

It's a very simple concept that actually works, and oddly enough, this self-discovery journey is quite fun too. It all begins with you. To trust your heart, your gut, and those butterflies in your tummy, it's important to get to know yourself first. I said it before, and I'll say it again, I think chillin' by yourself is important. Like really important. No book, podcast, or course can teach what life experience can. Just like any other relationship, the one with yourself takes time to develop.

Now when my body tells me something, I have a bit more optimism, because I know on the surface what I'm about to do or say may appear frightening, but once I push past the initial fear, the opportunity hiding around the corner could be life-changing. You'll never feel 100% ready. Ever. But I encourage you to try. Do it for the love of the possibilities because if there was ever a moment to follow your passion, that moment is now.

I spend a lot of time with myself to clear my head. Because when my head is clear, I make better life and career choices.

My high school experience, as daunting as it was, empowered me to think this way. As a victim of teen bullying, I spent so much time alone that it forced me to get real with myself and plan an escape route from my misery.

I ended up totally bombing high school.

I don't recall ever achieving a single 'A' (or even a 'B') except in gym. There's no way Dad would let me get away with not killin' it in the gym because I grew up playing high-performance sports my entire life. However, I never understood why that same laser focus I had in the pool or on the field did not transfer into the classroom. I have not been diagnosed with a learning disability, but as a kid, I always knew I was a little different than the rest of my peers and my teachers never failed to remind me.

I first realized this in fifth grade when I couldn't keep up with my small reading group and found it very difficult to comprehend the books we read in class. So, I skimmed the pages just to appear as if I completed my chapters for the week, knowing full well I did not, and was often mute during discussions, feeling like the dumbest in the room. I passed the sixth, seventh, and the eight grades—barely. Then I entered high school feeling like it could be a new beginning for me. Everyone shared my mixed feelings of nervousness and excitement, so I thought it was a level playing field. And my grades were okay in ninth grade, despite some personal challenges. However, I would not call grades 10 through 12 a success.

The struggle was so real. You probably experienced summers hanging with friends, attending pool parties, going on camping trips, and hosting BBQs. I spent my summer weeks in summer school (and night school too).

Some people might say that I didn't apply myself, that I'm lazy, and that's why I didn't succeed in school. I know a few of you reading this book will be quick to judge. That's fine. But what I really hope you take away from this is that not everyone who has failing grades has the intention of throwing their life away. In fact, I don't think that's the case for most of us. Speaking for myself, I raised my hand in class, paired with study buddies, and asked questions. I did try, and somehow, I still fell through the cracks.

I'll never forget one day at summer school when my teacher was handing back our English tests and blurted out loud, "Pauleanna, was this difficult for you?"

I get teary-eyed just thinking about it. Believe it or not, teachers embarrassed me more than you could imagine, with their sassy comments and bullshit excuses as to why their teaching methods did not match my learning style.

Now that I'm older, I've discovered new things about myself, like I'm a visual learner. Once I graduated, I started studying my learning style and applying it to my life and career goals. My dream career since I was a little girl was to be a professional writer. Many people, teachers and loved ones included, said that this was not possible for me. They said that my poor grades simply did not set me up for career success. So, I detoured and settled for a college program that my parents selected only to fall deeper into my depression.

Parents think they know what is best for you, but that's not always the case. Sometimes they will make decisions rooted in their own fears and insecurities. When I look back at it, I see that the tough love was the best kind because it forced me to put up a fight, but in the moment, I couldn't see that far ahead. I questioned everything and just couldn't settle on the fact that all these adults thought they knew my destiny and could paint that picture for me. Listen to me, when you decide what your dream is, fight for it, by any means necessary.

Learn to say, "Thanks for the advice, but I'm good."

You'll beef with your parents, but you have to remain in control. They are entitled to their opinion, and you have every right to look past it.

I've lived with depression and anxiety most of my life, and my triggers include people thinking that they think they know me better than I know myself. My attendance records in college were bad because I spent a lot of time at home in bed. When I did go to school, I was walking into a class where I didn't feel inspired. I didn't care what the teacher was saying, and all I could think about was the bigger world of opportunity I was missing outside my window. A diploma in Office Administration didn't light me up. For some of my classmates, it did. In fact, quite a few of them loved the program, but I didn't share the same enthusiasm.

I dropped out my second year after a suicide attempt. My world was filled with people, yet I still felt alone. My only company was the reflections of my past. I held them nightly. I often woke up in a cold sweat with only my anxiety laying on the pillow beside me. It all left me feeling stuck in the gray, somewhere between success and failure. Somewhere between good and great.

One day, I finally gained the courage to make the great escape at the subway stop, leaning over the edge of the forbidden yellow line. That morning I kissed my parents, my brother, and sister goodbye. When they asked me if I was okay, like many times before, I told them I was fine. (Side note: When I tell you I'm fine, I really mean I'm not. For years, I was drowning in depression, but no one ever cared to ask why. Instead, I was judged for being different and different is not accepted.) As the train approached, I closed my eyes and held my breath. People screamed. Lights flashed. But amongst the chaos, God revealed himself to me for the first time, as if to say that I wasn't allowed to throw my gift onto the tracks like trash. That I was a treasure and I just didn't know it yet.

After mentally and emotionally coming to terms with a second chance at life, I took it very seriously. I now knew I had a purpose and set out on a journey to discover what it was. I remember it vividly. I walked into my classroom, sat down for the exam, and decided that this wasn't for me. I actually came to this conclusion several months prior but had enough once the teacher handed me the test paper. So, I ripped it up, rose from my desk, and walked out towards the glimmer of light under the door which represented freedom. Was I scared out of my mind? Of course, I was. I had no strategy. I was just happy to do things on my terms. I don't have all the answers, but the best way I know how to climb out of any hole is gradually. The next step is always the step worth taking.

Now, I definitely don't want to make it seem like making that move meant the end of my anxiety. Believe me, it hasn't. It's still something I constantly have to work at, especially as an entrepreneur. Because entrepreneurship and mental illness often end up crossing paths. I read this dope article by Jessica Bruder in Fast Company a while back, called "The psychological price of Entrepreneurship." I read this paragraph and thought, damn, it's like she's writing about me:

"Successful entrepreneurs achieve hero status in our culture. We idolize the Mark Zuckerbergs and the Elon Musks. And we celebrate the blazingly fast growth of the Inc. 500 companies. But many of those entrepreneurs... harbor secret demons: Before they made it big, they struggled through moments of near-debilitating anxiety and despair—times when it seemed everything might crumble."

So real. When I walked out of that classroom and into life as an entrepreneur, I left behind the depression of not doing what I wanted and stepped into the anxiety of not knowing what was coming next. Chasing my dreams meant constantly stepping out on faith and hoping that there would be something for my foot to land on. It meant taking risks and hoping for the best possible outcome. And knowing that I could completely fail—and I sometimes—did didn't help. Bruh, that's like a recipe for anxiety. But I'm getting through it every day because I'm doing something that I love. I'd rather fail a thousand times in business than go back to failing in classrooms and jobs that made life feel unbearable.

But looking back, I can see how those moments pushed me to new levels. Had I not experienced that, I probably would still be trying to figure out 'what was wrong with me.' Instead, I've figured out what's right, what type of learner I am, and how to make adjustments. Allow your difficulties to redirect your steps. There's always a hidden blessing and benefit in every circumstance. Success is not just reserved for the elite. For anyone who has gone through the struggle like I have, please know that you can get a piece of it too.

Andrew

When I first started the O Agency, doubters showed up from everywhere. I can't entirely blame them. From the outside looking in, I must've seemed like a crazy person. After I graduated from Hampton, I got a job with Pepsi working in their sales department. There I was, right in the middle of corporate America. The job paid well, it was with a well-known company, and there was room for me to grow.

But it wasn't where I wanted to be. It wasn't all I wanted, and I knew that no matter how sweet the gig was with Pepsi, I wanted my own thing. I had tasted entrepreneurship back in college, I fell in love with branding, and I knew that staying at my corporate 9-to-5 wasn't what I needed.

I was ready to quit about six months in. But I had a mentor who told me to wait it out. And unlike the friends and family who really didn't understand, she wasn't telling me to stay at Pepsi 'cause it was cushy. She helped me see that staying there for at least a year would look good on my resume and give me some time to build an additional foundation for my business.

So, that's what I did. Every day, I showed up at the office. I'd work 12-hour days then head to Hampton to DJ the ball games. Then it was an hour and a half drive back home to hit the books. I spent my evenings studying books, courses, YouTube videos, and Google Academy on marketing, branding, entrepreneurship, and running a business. I did it in a small apartment while slurping back ramen noodles for most meals.

Yeah, I had a decent paycheck coming in from Pepsi, but I was eating Ramen and sleeping on the floor. This lasted for my entire first year out of college. It was tough, not because I had to, but because I didn't have to. The amount of self-discipline it took to make those sacrifices is the real definition of "laser-like focus" that a lot of people talk about but don't really understand.

You're probably thinking, "Man, that is crazy." Yeah, and I heard that a lot. And it was rough. Eating instant noodles and sleeping for 3-4 hours a day was hard enough without the people in my ear who thought I should just settle because I was living "the dream."

Friends and family, some of the people closest to me, hit me with more doubt and criticism than I could have expected. It was brutal. On top of trying to keep my mindset positive in the face of my new 24/7 hustle, I had to try and keep the negativity of people around me from leaking in and pulling me down.

That's why I completely agree with Pauleanna's advice about avoiding negative people. To get where I am, I had to put some space between myself and the people who just didn't get it.

You've got to do that too. Whether your critics can't understand why you won't just get a "real" job, or they think you should have your life together by now, that energy is bad news. And you can't waste time falling into that and getting caught up in their opinions. If you focus on what they think and want for your life, what happens to what you think and want? Nothing good. Like my good friend Alex Wolf says, trying to get everyone to love you will only make you hate yourself.

I think one of the most amazing parts of getting older is that moment when you finally realize that nobody can decide your place in the world but you. There's a point when you recognize that even if you're not one hundred percent sure of where you want to be or what you want to do, the decisions on that are still all yours to make. It's the most liberating thing. You stop worrying about other people's opinions, circumstances, and stress, and the picture of what you really want gets a little bit clearer.

But let's get real for a minute and address an uncomfortable truth. Sometimes, the negative person you need to distance yourself from is you. The version of you that's too busy worrying about where you should have been and what you should have done to focus on making moves now. The version of you that's so obsessed with watching other people glow up on Instagram that you're not even giving yourself a chance to discover how to shine.

One of the things I did when I decided that I needed to hustle for a dream bigger than a corporate office, was to get rid of distractions. Anything that made me feel like I wasn't enough or I wasn't focusing on the right things had to go. Anything that made me worry about what other people were doing instead of staying in my lane, I got rid of it. For a few years, I didn't even have a TV. I didn't need it taking up time or making me question my goals and my work. There's a reason they say that comparison is the thief of joy. Every time you focus on what other people are doing, you distract yourself from working on you, whether consciously or subconsciously. There are three simple things you can do to stop letting comparison make you your own worst bully.

Social media is all talk and no substance. Filter it out.

Social media is a blessing and a curse, especially Instagram. I've made some amazing connections over IG, but I've also seen how it can cripple people into self-doubt. Everyone stunts for the 'gram. We see the influencers with the luxury cars, living the jet set life. But we don't know what it took for them to get there, or if any of that is even real. A lot of that Instagram glamour is fake, and most people are broke. Let's just call it like it is. I know this because our agency works with a lot of influencers who want to monetize and grow a business, yet have an ego based on followers with no real value proposition.

I've worked with extremely successful and wealthy people who hardly have an Instagram following. And we all know that there are people out there with more followers than dollars and more likes than successes. You just can't use social media to measure success.

Now, I'm not saying don't get on social media. I'm on every platform. I've connected with some really cool people online. But every time I log in, I'm on there with blinders. I'm not getting dazzled by the flossing and the stunting. I see quality. I see opportunities to make good connections. I'm searching for the gems of information. And I don't ever let flashy pics and boastful captions make me feel like what I'm doing isn't enough.

So, if you're going to be on social media, use it to level up instead of letting other people's highlight reels pull you down. A lot of really cool entrepreneurs share their expertise right on Instagram. Kendall Kyndall, John Henry, and Regina Anajienou are just a few who drop gems in their videos, captions, and stories. Get on that. Fill up your timeline with people who will help you learn and grow, and maybe even figure out what you want to do. And log out sometimes. The world isn't going to end if you're not scrolling your timeline.

Believe it or not, you've already won.

I'm not on Elon Musk's level yet. And man, I'd like to be. But I don't let that discourage me. Instead of comparing myself to other successful people, I compare myself to the old versions of me. I think about the Andrew who was cutting hair in his dorm room. Or the Andrew that was living in his car. Or the Andrew that had nothing to his name but $80 at

18. Even when I was living in a small apartment and hustling to get my business off the ground, I was past those struggles. And I always stayed grateful for that. I'm where I'm at because I worked hard and stayed focused. That keeps me going and stops me from being distracted by other people's wins.

Whenever you're tempted to give into the idea that you're not good enough or you don't measure up, take a minute to think about what you have done. Seriously, stop and write it down if you have to.

You're underestimating yourself because you still care what other people think.

Doubt doesn't get things done. And if you go into situations thinking that you're not enough, you're going to miss the mark every time. I did one of my first branding projects for a friend of mine at Hampton. He was a fitness instructor and wanted to grow his business. So, I told him I'd help him make it happen. I didn't have a degree in marketing. I didn't have some long resume of successful projects to show him. It would have been easy to talk myself out of stepping up and taking him on. But, I went in with confidence that I had enough skills and helped him plan and pull off a successful tour.

So, if you've given yourself credit for your progress, then you know what you're already capable of. It's time to start realizing how much more you have in you. It's cool if you're not sure what you want yet, but it's unacceptable to be out here thinking you don't have something good to contribute to the world. I read an interview with Cam Newton a while ago, and he laid out the keys to success. He said something like, "I was already a starting quarterback in my mind. I was already a Super Bowl winner in my mind. I really believed that I was extremely successful even before I accomplished it." It's so simple, but that's the answer to getting out of your own way. It goes right back to that mindset I was talking about. When you start recognizing your potential for greatness, anything is possible.

LIVING THAT ENTRY-LEVEL LIFE

Pauleanna

The biggest challenge for visual thinkers is how to get the images out of our heads and into the real world. The solution that worked for me is blogging and making use of social media. But I had to build my career alongside working a job. Yes, a job. I know that's a shocker. I do think volunteering and gaining employment is one of the best stepping stones to helping you figure things out.

One of my favorite career books is I Shouldn't Be Telling You This. It's written by Kate White. In the chapter titled 'What Are You Really Lusting For?,' she says, "If you haven't found your calling yet, the best thing to do is to get your butt off your chair, fill your life with a wide array of unusual experiences, and allow yourself to bump into what will exhilarate you." I agree with her a million percent. You have to try your hand at different things to know what you like and don't like. After college, I had no money. Getting a job was inevitable. But I didn't complain because I knew it was only temporary. That's the thing. Everything in life is. I wish more people could see beyond the limits of their circumstances because then they'd make moves that benefitted them long-term.

Yes, you may hate your job, but please understand that this season of your life has importance. The reason why you are not happy in your current situation is that you're not trying to find the beauty in your world of chaos. Not only are you not trying to see the beauty through your lens, but your narrow-sightedness is delaying your blessings. The more you speak negativity into your life, the higher you build a wall between you and your destiny. Words have enormous power, and if you don't start filtering your language and talking to yourself with more respect, you'll keep walking in circles. You may feel like a mess but take a page from all the people we look up to. The one common thread they share is that positive thinking is always at the forefront of each of their success stories.

Try your best, not anyone else's.

Not just some days, but every day. Because it's really silly to ask for more (money, opportunity, success) when you haven't even mastered less. Have big dreams and ideas, but don't expect more blessings if you can't master your current situation. Be excellent right where you are. You and everyone else has to start at zero. If you want to be a success, there are levels to this. I don't care where you work. If you're

- flippin' burgers at McDonald's
- washing dishes at Burger King
- sorting mail at the post office
- operating coat check at the club
- working customer service at the bank

It doesn't matter. You make sure you are the best at what you do and show others what you've got. You don't know who's watching and what power they hold. I also know how much you despise your position, but consider this practice for the big win. At every stage and every age, you need to be productive. Master this season so you can take the lesson and move on.

My first job out of college, I worked as a receptionist at an interior design firm, a very prestigious multi-million dollar company. My boss, Gino, was an older Italian man who yelled at me daily. Honestly, I think that's just the way he spoke. Loud and proud. But it scared me to death. I had just started navigating the working world and could barely stand on my own two feet. Sometimes, you could even find me in the bathroom crying on the floor. I can't even begin to describe how much I despised my boss. I wanted to quit but was even too scared to do that. Until one day I did. I told Gino I found a new position and I was leaving.

Yeah, right.

He told me to sit down, and that I wasn't going anywhere. Then he asked me my price. I replied, "If you can match my new job, I will think about staying, but the real reason I'm leaving is because I don't think I can handle this environment." Gino looked back at me with a puzzled expression on his face, but quickly understood what I meant. For the first time, we had a heart to heart. He told me that I was young enough to be his granddaughter and that he was hard on me because he could tell I was built for challenge. He wanted to build my character and told me that if I ever wanted to be as successful as him, I needed to develop tougher skin.

From that point forward, I changed the way I viewed my 9-to-5 and all the jobs I held afterward. Instead of complaining about your job, try changing your perspective. For me, going to work was like going to business school for free. While I continued at that job, I didn't cry a single tear after that conversation with Gino. Although he continued yelling at me, I had an easier time shaking it off because I never forgot what he told me. "If I ever wanted to be as successful as him I needed to build tougher skin." So, every single day, I studied the company. We were a small but strong team, so I was able to have my hands in a bit of everything. It was my first bite of the business world, and I was hooked.

I later moved on to work as an assistant to c-level executives in a variety of industries like finance, consulting, media, and retail which afforded me the opportunity to see how a major corporation runs. Your 9-to-5 doesn't have to stunt your growth. In fact, it can accelerate it. Your success will only be as big as your appetite, which means you will need vision to get through this.

Andrew

If you're a millennial and you're unsure what to do with your life, don't be too hard on yourself. That's pretty normal. You're young, your experience is limited, and it's hard to make a decision that big when you don't know all the options.

Just get out there and do something.

When I first got to Hampton, I knew I needed to do something about my almost-empty bank account. So, I slapped a sign up on my dorm room door, pulled out my Dad's old barber tools, and started giving $5 haircuts to my classmates. Technically, that was my first business though that wasn't really the plan. Being a barber was never some big aspiration I had or something I felt destined to do. It was just an opportunity to make money using what I had on hand.

While I was running my dorm room barbershop, I found out that the campus DJ, DJ Tay, was a senior and graduating soon. I had absolutely no DJ experience whatsoever, but I love music, and I saw a chance to try something new. So, I reached out to him and told him I wanted to DJ. I wasn't a prodigy or anything. My first gig was mediocre. But I enjoyed it, and I decided to get good. I practiced, took feedback and direction from DJ Tay, and invested in my own DJ equipment. Soon, I was DJing several nights a week. I quit cutting hair because I was making way more spinning at parties, and I was enjoying it more too.

Between that first accidental business and where I am today, I've had a ton of other jobs including party promoter, a side hustle giving my college classmates advice on business branding, and an entry-level corporate job. From every single one of those jobs, I learned something valuable about myself. I learned to recognize what I liked and didn't like and what my natural skills and talents are. I went to college to get a degree in Pharmacology. Could you imagine if I'd let my first degree major decide my path for me instead of getting out there and getting new experiences? I wouldn't be here living a life I love.

So, if you're undecided, or if the thing you're studying at school doesn't feel like a reason to leap out of bed in the morning, get out there and test the waters. Volunteer, take a class or a course, sign up for a community activity or initiative. See a job opening that looks interesting, but it's outside of your field? Send in your resume anyway. You might be surprised to discover it's something you're really good at or actually enjoy. All of those experiences can help shape you.

No matter how good/smart/successful you get, know that you still have things to learn.

No position is too small to learn or grow from. Entry-level jobs give you a chance to get in at ground level and see how a business operates on the front line, just like Pauleanna did. You'll learn the ins and outs of customer service and sharpen your people skills. Yeah, the pay may not be amazing, but money isn't the only currency. If you give your best effort and pay attention, you'll pick up invaluable lessons that you'll use long after you've moved up in the company or moved on to something better. Consider it free research and development. You're getting paid to learn.

I'll give you a crazy example. I was watching that show on HGTV, Dirty Jobs, and there was a man on there who had a job as a garbage collector. That's one of those jobs that a lot of people look at and scorn because, well, it's dirty. You pick up trash bins and ride around on a truck that smells bad. There's nothing glamorous about it, and it definitely doesn't seem like anything to brag about. But that man gave that job his absolute all. He showed up every day on time, built relationships with the people on his route, and was the best garbage collector possible. Today, he's the owner of his own trash collection company. If that's not a living example of 'started from the bottom,' I don't know what is.

If any of this is sounding scary for you, let me offer you a perspective shift. A lot of people are afraid to try things and explore possibilities because they're worried that they'll be "wasting time." They're stressing about trying something new and failing because they think that will keep them from getting to the thing they're going to succeed at. If that sounds like you, consider this: you've been told that life is short, so you don't have time for trial and error.

But that's crap. Life is long. You've got years ahead of you. Literal decades.

Obsession with always being right is a mind f*ck.

Both Pauleanna and I decided the majors we went to college for weren't right. We both worked multiple jobs in different industries. Our early twenties were filled with trial and error. Now, we're both living our dreams because we gave ourselves permission to try the things we wanted and figure out what made sense for us.

So, worse case scenario, you spend a few months or a year in an entry-level job, only to find out it isn't what you want to do. Or you take a course that bores you half to death. Or you start a business idea that turns out to be a total fail. Okay, take the lessons and skills and move on to the next thing. I promise you that you have time. Give yourself space and time to discover who you are, what you do well, and what you want out of life. At the end of the day, the only thing you need to do is get up every day and keep pushing. I had a conversation with Tola Lawal, and I think her favorite quote is one you need to know and remember. She said, "'Every morning in Africa, a lion wakes up and knows it must run faster than the slowest gazelle or it will starve.

It doesn't matter whether you're the lion or the gazelle, every morning you better be running.' It's actually a sports reference, from Christopher McDougall, and he said it in one of these books where he was talking about racing. And I was just like that shit applies to life no matter what. No matter whether you're the hunter or the hunted. Get up and run every single day."

Chapter 2:
What Makes You Say "Hell Nah"

THE MOST POWERFUL WORD IN THE ENGLISH LANGUAGE

Pauleanna

Once in a while, it really hits people that they don't have to experience life in the way they have been told to. When you discover who you are and what you want, something magical happens, and you create a space where bullshit and negativity simply cannot exist. You break the rules, create your own path and never look back. This is where I am at in my life today. If you haven't crossed over to the other side, the thought seems scary, I know. But you have to go through your fear to experience your breakthrough.

But I feel the need to express how important it is to do things at your own pace, according to your own agenda. Don't succumb to the pressure and expectations of other people. I have a problem with people of authority like parents, teachers, government officials and others who feel like we're supposed to, without question, have our lives planned out down to the very last detail, according to their timelines. Because guess what? Despite all the advice outlined in this book, some people will still take forever and a day to get their lives figured out, and that's okay. This is not a race. This is not a game. This is our lives. I believe that this is a time where life is meant to be lived. It's a time of evolution. Whether we figure things out in our 20s or that uncertainty rolls into our 30s, it shouldn't take away from the fact that everyone is born with a purpose and people will turn this key at different points. Forget what other people say, because at the end of the day, what really matters is you. The key is to identify what's important to you and eliminate everything else because working on a better you is time well spent.

Look, if people don't get it, it's not your issue. Don't let someone who has done nothing tell you how to do anything. Bad advice is more common than you think, which is why it is so important to weed it out. What I've learned growing up is that you have to be bold enough to use your own voice and be brave enough to listen to your heart. Intuition is very real, and you shouldn't ignore it because when you learn to follow your heart, you will always know what is "best" for you.

Do what feels right, even if it feels risky.

My dream to become a writer was clear when I was in elementary school, but between elementary school and college, many people told me I would never make money from my writing. If I had low levels of self-awareness, then I probably would have believed them, but what they didn't know is that I spend an insane amount of time working on myself. As a result, I am completely in tune with my intuition, which has also helped in other areas of my life, by the way.

I'll tell you a quick story.

Most people don't know this, but I was engaged when I was 25. I was with a man who I thought was the love of my life. After five months, we decided that we wanted to take the next step in our lives together and soon we were picking out diamond rings and matching wedding bands. I was excited to finally be fulfilling my dreams of becoming a wife and mother. I cared for my man, deeply. More than you'll ever know. But the faster we moved forward, the more I pulled back.

My intuition.

It was telling me something.

I could not ignore it.

I confided in many other couples whom I looked up to. I told them how I was feeling. But they didn't listen. They said, "Just do it. He's a good man from a good family with a stable career. What more do you want? Your feelings are natural. You are just nervous." I replied, "Nahhhhh. This is not nervousness. It's different."

Sadly, I knew in my heart that he was not my forever. The intuition was very real, and I knew it was not wise to ignore it. So, I didn't. I broke up with him, and as hard as it was to leave and as much as I loved him, I loved me more.

Let's fast forward to a few short years ago. Suddenly, my ex started following me again on Instagram and reached out to meet up. The confident side of me said, "Maybe he wants to rekindle our romance. Why wouldn't he, I'm fine as hell."

No, really. I'm a catch. Don't hate.

But all joking aside, I agreed to meet up with him and hear him out. After all, it had been at least two years since we last spoke. I was curious about his well-being. We met at a cute restaurant downtown. I was greeted with his warm smile. For a moment, I felt special. I felt all kinds of mixed feelings.

But only for a moment. Let's not get too ahead of ourselves.

We dived into a great conversation. I lit up hearing about how well his career was going and his plans for personal and professional growth. It's always refreshing to see a man with a plan. That was one of the unique qualities that attracted me to him in the first place. But the conversation turned left when his voice got softer. Real quiet. Nervous, even.

He said, "I'm engaged."

I said, "Oh, congrats. That's great." And I meant it sincerely. I knew he was not my forever. I made that decision years prior, so my reaction was completely genuine.

A murmur followed, ".... to a man."

I blinked once. I blinked twice. Then smiled. But behind this smile was a huge, "What in the hell?" So, I asked him to repeat it just to be clear. He confirmed.

I took a breath and said, "Okay." That was the only word that could escape my lips.

"Okay."

After taking a second to process this information. I took another breath, smiled and asked all the who, what, when, where, and hows.

He was completely upfront and honest. Open. Vulnerable. I will keep those details sacred. Oddly enough, in those moments, I appreciated him even more. My mood quickly shifted from angry to compassionate and supportive. He didn't need someone to judge him. After wrapping up our talk. We hugged goodbye and left the restaurant in two different directions. I haven't spoken to him since.

That, right there, is the secret. My gut feeling tells me everything, whether it was leaving my ex, leaving school, or distancing myself from friends. My gut has never steered me in the wrong direction. I've learned to trust it even when I don't understand it. I didn't find out until two years later what it was really trying to say. You have to learn how to silence the noise and ask yourself if the advice you're receiving is the best version of it. I am very happy for my ex. I hope he lives happily ever after with his new partner. But I can't help but think what would have happened had I ignored the whisper, the signs that told me to make a left instead of a right. The entire course of my life could be different right now.

Here's another thought, set boundaries.

Stick to your principles.

My biggest mistake growing up was listening to people who thought they knew me better than I knew myself. This is what led to a downward spiral. Once I learned that not all people and things deserve my time, life became a lot clearer. So now I am very selective about who I choose to open up to or listen to.

I'm writing some of my parts of this book from Hoboken, New Jersey. Andrew and I are locked away in an Airbnb writing the draft of this manuscript. The funny thing is before meeting Andrew in December of 2016, I must have been asked a million times over, "When are you going to write your next book?" Since publishing my first novel in March 2014, there was an immediate expectation from my audience that I would birth another one right after.

I'm going into the fourth-year anniversary of Everything I Couldn't Tell My Mother in a few months, which tells you that I was in no rush. But instead of people letting me chill and pursue other dreams and goals, I constantly had to deal with all kinds of criticism. From family members calling me a one-hit wonder to the pressure in media interviews questioning why the sequel isn't out, it damn near drove me crazy and turned me off from the entire process. But I play for the long game, and my gut told me to chill, live my life, meet new people, and wait on the green light. Of course, I could have written another book. I have some colleagues who have produced four or five books in the time I was able to produce one. But I am not in a race with anyone. The only competition I've got is the person I see when I look into the mirror.

When I released my book in 2014, I was happy, but exhausted. It took me four years to write, and it's a body of work that I am extremely proud of. But once the applause faded and the hype went away, I replayed so many voices in my head.

But I've been trying to stay in my lane and remain focused on what I want. Even though their criticism mounted on top of my own thoughts made the last few years kinda rough, I am happy I stood firm and didn't let them dictate my next steps. Had I not held out as long as I did, this project would not exist.

Social media is the modern day "keeping up with the Joneses."

I met Andrew at a conference in Washington, DC and almost instantly we knew that we wanted to work together. We just weren't entirely sure in what capacity. Over the course of a few months, we got to know each other really well and realized we were more similar than we were different. The Build Your Own Brand Society was an idea he shared with me during one of our brainstorming sessions. From that conversation, our partnership was born. Andrew would lead the movement, be the face, and build the brand strategy, and I would support him by filling the gaps, starting with becoming the editorial director of the blog platform and managing our team of contributors. That position led me here, writing to you and developing the book that was deep within me but was waiting for the right time. Anything before this moment wouldn't have been my best work because I have never been more inspired than I am now.

PARENTAL GUIDANCE

Andrew

I know parents always mean well when they tell us what to do with our lives. I mean, that's what they're used to. From the time we were little, they've been teaching us how to live life. They taught us even the most basic things like how to dress and feed ourselves. I guess it's understandable that they would just go on thinking they need to tell us how to live.

But there comes a point where we're old enough to know what's best for us. The problem is we usually realize that long before our parents do. By the time we hit 17 or 18, we start to get an idea of how we want our lives to look. Meanwhile, our parents have planned our weddings, named our children, and decided on our careers, and a lot of them don't even think to ask us what we want.

While we can delay the marriage and babies talk for a bit, parents can be super pushy about careers. For millennials, this can be really tricky to navigate because our parents define success so differently than we do. The idea of making millions as a tech founder, brand consultant, social media influencer, motivational speaker, travel writer or any of the crazy ventures our generation has created seems unbelievable to them because it just didn't exist in their day. For a lot of our parents, success means a "safe, practical job" in law, medicine or business with a good salary, great benefits, and three weeks of vacation every year.

If you're a child of immigrants, that pressure is doubled. Immigrant parents are so serious about the "American dream." And if you decide to go your own way, it can be brutal. I can tell you that because I lived it. The decision to chase my own vision pretty much ruined my relationship with my family.

My parents came to America from Vietnam before I was born. They had very little money and barely spoke English, but they knew they wanted their children to have a better chance at life than they did back home. They worked hard to give me every opportunity to succeed. And by succeed, they meant get a degree in Pharmacology and become a pharmacist or a doctor. There was no plan B in their minds. That was it.

That's how I ended up at Hampton. It was one of the only universities with a 6-year Pharmacology program. My first semester, I went to my classes and sat through the lectures, but my head wasn't in it. I failed almost every single class. I didn't want to spend 8+ hours a day in a white lab coat counting pills and dealing with prescriptions. In my parents' eyes, that was winning. To me, it was death by boredom. So, after that first semester, I made the crazy decision to change my major...without telling my parents.

For months, I said nothing to them. Keeping that secret was like torture. Every chance they got, they were telling people how proud they were that their son was in pharmacy school. Whenever we ran into people we knew, they started talking about it. All I could do was stand there and nod, too afraid to tell them the truth. I just kept imagining how disappointed they would be. I knew they wouldn't understand.

I finally worked up the courage to tell them over the phone. I called home and told my Dad that I really wanted to start my own business and that I had changed my degree program to an MBA. He was so mad. He told me he felt like I'd thrown away everything he groomed me for to chase a dream, but if I was getting an MBA, I might as well come home and get it at an in-state university instead of spending all the money to get my degree out-of-state.

But Hampton was part of my vision for my life. In that first year, that school became about way more than an education. It was full of culture and community. It was full of opportunities. I'd started my DJ gig and my barber business, built friendships and made connections. So, when my father told me I could either move back home or be cut off, I chose Hampton.

It was one of those crazy moments where you make a tough choice knowing the consequences are gonna suck, but you don't realize just how bad until it hits. I remember it like yesterday how my father's response cut me. My Vietnamese isn't great, but I understood him perfectly when he said, "I'm disowning you."

I was on my own.

I went through so many emotions and thoughts. I had just lost my relationships with my family, and on top of that, I had no idea how I was going to pay for my next semester of school. I made a massive leap, and I had nothing to fall back on. The reality of what I chose hit me hard. I couldn't afford housing, so I slept in my car or crashed on friends' couches. When I needed to come up with the money for school, my jobs weren't cutting it, and I couldn't get a loan without a co-signer, so I joined the Army. I didn't tell my parents about enlisting until the day before I shipped out for boot camp because I had accepted that all I had was me, God, and my dream.

I don't want you to think I don't feel bad for the way things went with my parents. I didn't want to disappoint them or make them feel like I didn't value their sacrifice. I just knew I couldn't live my life in the shadow of their expectations. I was willing to walk away from my relationship with them to do what I felt I needed to do.

Of course, I realize that's not the path for everybody. Going against your parents is hard and losing your relationship with them is even worse. That's why my first advice to people dealing with this dilemma isn't to do what I did. I think there are ways that you can work around it to try to do what's best for you and still keep things cool with your parents.

There is ALWAYS a solution if you're creative.

Just like you would negotiate a business deal or a better salary, try to work out an arrangement that still pleases your parents. Sometimes there's a middle ground you can get them to agree on. You could ask them to give you a year or two to try things your way, and if it doesn't work out, do what they want. That might motivate you to work even harder because now you have a time limit you have to meet. See if you can find a way to do both things — get the degree they want you to have while you spend your spare time studying your craft and honing your skills. Again, you'll have to work harder, and sacrifice chill time and Netflix binges (and really, you should be cutting those back anyway), but at least everybody gets what they want.

What if that doesn't work? Then you're at the same crossroad I was at ten years ago. It's time to decide if you're willing to go it alone, with no safety net, no financial backing, and no family support. You've gotta decide if you're willing to jump. But the advice I'd give you that I didn't have ten years ago is to take the time to get ready to make that leap.

Prepare for the worst and there's a good chance it'll never happen.

Just like how you shouldn't just quit your job without knowing how you're going to pay your next month's rent, you shouldn't tell your parents you're just going to do you without a plan to survive the aftermath. Not having an exit plan is why I ended up sleeping curled up on couches, the back seat of my car, and an Army-issued sleeping bag.

Give yourself a timeline and start taking steps to make your move. Lay low and follow your parents' rules while you start saving the money you'll need to take care of yourself. Find a job (or two or three) that will help you make ends meet. Spend your time building your network, sharpening your skills, and learning as much as you can about whatever it is you're planning to do. I'm not saying having this exit plan means making that break will be easy, but being prepared makes it a little less scary.

However you choose to navigate this issue, just know that you'll be good. If you choose to reach a compromise, execute an exit plan, or stick it out until you're older, you have time. Remember what I said about life being long earlier? It's true here too. Reaching a compromise with your parents or waiting until you have the independence to do your own thing may mean having to wait longer for your dream, but that doesn't mean you can't still get there. Don't discourage yourself by thinking that because you've got to wait a few years that your goal is doomed.

The same is true if you go for it right off the bat. Take it from me, when you make that move, there are definitely going to be moments of failure and frustration. When you screw up, it's going to feel like the end of the world at first. I know how easy it is to want to give in to that. Don't. Failure just means you've got to get up and figure out how to tackle things differently. It took me ten years of struggling, screwing up, and adjusting to get to where I am. Had I given up after that first night curled up in the backseat of my car, I don't know if I'd have any of the things I do now. But every time things went wrong, I focused on how much time I had to get it right and that paid off.

I'm still sorry that I disappointed my parents, but I really would do it all again because I know one day I'm going to make them proud. I still go as hard as I do to show them that I did make the right decision. I'm going to prove to them that I didn't throw away what they worked for, I just found a different path to success — my own.

Chapter 3:
Kick Convention to the Curb

GO BEYOND THE DEGREE

Andrew

The amazing thing about success is that there are about a thousand different ways to get there. I, Pauleanna, and thousands of successful entrepreneurs like Regina Anaejionu and Ivan Land Jr. have all found our own ways to win that didn't fit the path people expected us to take. There's nothing wrong with the conventional path. We still need people who define success the way our parents do. We need doctors, lawyers, and accountants. We can't all be unconventional entrepreneur types. But one of the things I love most about this generation, you know, the people who are willing to work hard and grind for what we want, is that we recognize that we can color outside the lines. We're creating our own jobs or changing the way that existing ones work. We don't let ourselves be squeezed by the rules and standards. We do things our own way. We're creative, innovative, rule breakers. Knowledge is still the thing that makes the world go 'round, but college degrees and internships aren't the only way to learn anymore.

I finished my MBA at Hampton, and it taught me a lot about owning and operating a business, but I didn't study marketing in school. Everything I know about branding, the bread and butter of my first successful business, I learned on my own. I gained all that knowledge in two ways: studying resources and straight up experience. Ten thousand hours worth of it. What does that tell you? I'm not smarter than you, just dedicated and obsessed with improvement. I dare you to calculate 10,000 hours and study your craft for that long. You'll be the hottest thing on the block.

The resources you need to learn exist, you just need to set your own course.

We live in the age of information, and everything you've ever wanted to know about just about anything can be found if you're looking for it. If there's something you're interested in, there are tons of resources out there, some of them free. Books, magazines, podcasts, YouTube videos, and blogs are available, and you don't have to spend a fortune. You do have to spend time and discipline. College makes it a bit easier by providing the information for you and a schedule to learn and test it, but when you're learning on your own, you have to seek out the info and commit yourself to taking it in.

It's cool if you start with the stuff everyone else is reading and watching. Everybody has to learn the basics. Just make sure you're putting in the work to actually study and learn it. It's easy to slack when nobody is telling you what to do and when to do it. You have to discipline yourself. If you've got a day job or you're in school, make time in the evenings, on the weekends, and during your commute to study up on your craft or interest.

When I first graduated from Hampton, I had three jobs. I had a corporate sales gig at Pepsi, I was still DJing, and I had the O Agency in its earliest stage. I needed to dig in and really learn about branding, but man, my schedule was hectic. The 9-to-5 was really a 6-to-6, I was spinning in the evenings, and by the time I got home, it was late at night. It would have been so easy to just fall into bed and study "later." But I'd force my eyes open and get to reading or watching. I'm obsessed with Shark Tank. I think anyone who wants to be an entrepreneur should be. Back then, I watched every single episode of every single season in every single country. And when those were done, I watched Dragons' Den (both the UK and the

Canadian editions). Watching Shark Tank and Dragons' Den taught me the art of talking about your business and pitching to investors. I learned what people expected a business owner to know and be able to talk about confidently. I learned from other people's mistakes, got creative ideas from other startups, and learned to think like a venture capitalist, all from two TV shows. It gave me a great starting point for getting my own pitch perfect.

Sometimes, I didn't get to bed until 2:00 am and had to be up again in a few hours for work. But I treated my learning the same way a good student treats university classes. I was laser-focused and super committed. Because I understood that it was an investment in my success, and it was really as simple as study or fail. And not just fail a little test, but fail at my business. Failing even though I tried my best is one thing. But failing because I was slacking off? Not an option.

If there's something you're interested in or a field you want to pursue, you have no excuse for being ignorant. Get your head in the books. Put your headphones in and listen to podcasts from successful people in your field. Study, study, study. You're up against people who went to school for the thing you're learning on your own, so you don't have room for being lazy.

If you don't really have a clue what to start reading, Alex Wolf has some great advice:

"Pay attention to what is happening in the economy if you care about making some money. When I say that, I mean, read Fast Company Magazine because Fast Company is all about practical innovation. Any publication that is going to talk about the direction the economy is going in is key. And when I say economy, I'm not saying look at stock market charts and stuff like that. I'm saying figure out what is going to be valuable in the marketplace. Are you going to need to know how to do this or that? You need to figure out what those things are because if you learn how to do them, you will be good. It won't matter so much about the degrees and stuff. People will just want to make sure you can make them money."

And you'll want to make money cause you don't really have room to be too cheap either. I'm not trying to be insensitive. I know how hard it is when cash is tight. You've read about my college days. You know I've been there. But at some point, it has to stop being an excuse for not investing in yourself. There's only so much you can learn from free resources.

You eventually have to start pouring some money into your goals.

For years, I ate ramen noodles and lived in a small apartment so that I could save money and invest in myself. I signed up for courses online, some of them costing thousands of dollars. Some of them were amazing. I got the chance to learn directly from marketing and branding experts who were killing it. Some of the things I learned in those courses were crazy valuable, and I'm still using them to this day. Really good courses pay for themselves times over if you take what you learn and apply it for your own success. I recommend platforms like General Assembly, Udemy, and Coursera.

Be prepared for courses that miss the mark.

Not every course is going to end up being valuable. There are tons of e-courses online, and some are better than others. But you can't let the fear of investing in a course that doesn't really pay off make you stingy. Just like with anything else you do, there are going to be hits and misses. Before you enroll in a course, do your research. Read any reviews you can find. Speak to people you know in the field or industry to see if they know if the course is reputable. Even if you can't talk to successful people in your industry, scan their blogs and social media to see if there are any courses that they recommend. If you're planning to take an e-course from an influencer or expert, read reviews and check out their free resources first to get a sense of the quality.

There's no way to absolutely guarantee you'll never waste money on a course that's not useful to you, but at least you can mitigate the risk. You can also go to byobsociety.com/education to get the full scope of our favorite vetted places to learn online.

One thing that helped me keep my perspective when I took a course that sucked was that I didn't look for an ROI in each individual decision. Rather, I chose to look for the ROI at the macro level. Was I moving forward in the right direction every six months? Was there progress being made, however fast or slow? That's my ROI. Most people get so caught up with immediate returns that they don't realize shit takes longer than they expect. And that's very natural for humans; we're overly optimistic. Ever heard someone say they're five minutes away, every 15 minutes? We as humans suck at estimating the future, and that's just the reality. Remember, think long-term.

What you can't learn online, you have to learn from experience.

The next best teacher, and maybe even a better one sometimes, is experience. I learned so much of my business knowledge from just trying things. Sometimes, I tried, and it worked out. Other times, I tried, and I failed, hard. That's just part of business. Nobody gets it all right off the bat. Failing is inevitable. There's a meme I saw recently that said, "That big win is behind that one failure." I think that's the problem with most people. They fail once and believe it should work the next time. It's unrealistic and the wrong attitude. Failure is an amazing teacher. I legit know that I'm only in the position I'm in today because my resume for failure is a lot longer than most people's. I've been trying and failing at things for a whole decade. That meme should say, "That big win is behind 1,000 failures." That should really put perspective on things for you. Now, how bad do you really want it?

I recently had a chat with Ivan Land Jr. the founder of a successful consulting and design company. He's been doing amazing things from the time he was a kid. At 13, he bought BeyonceKnowles.com and sold the domain name to her father. He's worked in the music industry and with massive brands like Google, Apple, and Complex Magazine. But while we were talking, he told me that his business almost tanked at one point. You wouldn't know it now because he's doing really well for himself, but he almost lost it all because there were some failures behind-the-scenes. But Ivan was able to learn from that failure and turn things around, and his business is still booming today.

If there's something you want to do or learn, don't stress because you're not studying it at school. You can learn anything, anywhere, anytime if you're willing to commit to it. Get out there and start reading, watching, and listening. Practice and try things, and let the mess-ups and the failures teach you. If you want it, it's yours. You just have to put in the work.

Pauleanna

I love that Andrew talks about failure as a learning tool because it's literally failure that taught me how I needed to learn. As I said before, I'm a visual learner. That means I don't learn like other people do. Back in high school, when the teachers would get up at the front of the class and just talk with no visual aids, my brain just checked out.

Bruh, it was stressful. All my classmates were getting it, and I was forever lost. I felt so slow and bad about myself until I had my Eureka moment. As a visual learner, I need ideas and information to be associated with images and techniques. Basically, I don't learn as much if people just talk at me. I think in pictures. This is why I'm obsessed with the game of chess (and yes, I'm actually good, in case you're wondering). It also explains why I'm able to tell stories in such vivid detail, or why what other people see as chaos makes perfect sense to me.

It took me four years of high school, two years of college, and so many failed classes before I finally figured it out. I honestly can't believe I had to figure it out on my own. But my life changed when I did. You see, my failing grades pushed me to new levels.

You have to figure out how you learn best.

If you're like me, and you struggle with school and conventional learning methods, then maybe you need to figure out why it is that things don't click. Maybe you're a visual learner like me, and you need to take your notes with little doodles or color coding or anything else that might make it stick. Or maybe you struggle with reading and retaining information. Maybe audiobooks or video content work better for you. Maybe you're a social learner, and you need to process information by interacting with other people. Whatever it takes for you to learn, do it. Ain't no shame in the game. This is your future we're talking about. Don't go trying to force yourself to fit into systems and methods that don't make sense for you. Your unique learning style is only a disadvantage if you don't cater to it. And if you're learning on your own, you have the upper hand because you get to set the pace and the method.

If you want to know something, Google that ish.

I'm a big believer in self-guided learning. I always tell people Google and YouTube are like free universities. If you want to learn something, just hit up the search bar and find it. You'd be amazed how much information is out there if you just look for it. And there's something really fulfilling about finding the answers for yourself, or maybe I'm just a nerd obsessed with learning. But if you're trying to be successful, you better get on that level. If you're not obsessed with learning about the thing you want to do with your life, I'm sorry, but there ain't no gentle way to say this: you're not going to make it.

I live in study mode every single day. I love listening to dynamic speakers like Susan Cain, Lisa Nichols, Tony Robbins, Eric Thomas, TD Jakes, and Joel Osteen. I study successful people like Jay-Z, Mindy Kaling, and Steve Stoute. If you see my headphones in, I'm probably listening to a podcast like School of Greatness, Boss Babe, or Hashtag & Stilettos. I've been doing this for years because I'm hungry and really want to learn and grow. No matter what level of success I reach, I keep pushing. It adds value to my life and puts me in a position to win because knowledge is power.

And I surround myself with people who think the same way and have the same habits. One of my good friends, Courtney Sanders, is the founder of women empowerment brand Think and Grow Chick. I recently interviewed her for Forbes, and she shared that while she was working her entry-level office job, she took on the tasks that nobody else wanted, like filing papers, so she could put her headphones in and listen to business podcasts and audiobooks. All that studying paid off because she made six figures off the side-hustle she built while working her corporate job, and now she's running that business full-time.

Honestly, no matter what career path you're choosing, whether you're going into entrepreneurship or the corporate world, learning how to find the answers for yourself is important. For one, when you put in the effort to learn things for yourself, you actually learn more. But it also makes people more inclined to help you if you can prove that you actually tried to get the answer for yourself before asking them.

As a person whose inbox is always full of questions about everything from business to mentorship, I can tell you, it looks better if you've tried. I don't say that because I don't want to answer questions. I love answering questions. I'm a mentor by profession. That's part of the job. But when people slide in my inbox or my DMs to ask me questions they could have easily found the answer to on Google, or even right on my website or social media, it makes me question how dedicated they are to their goals.

I give this advice so freely because I follow it myself. I have amazing mentors in my life. They're brilliant people who are super successful and rich in experience, relationships, opportunities and — let's not even be coy here — money. People who have that much going for them are always busy. So, even though I know I could pick up the phone and call my mentors or send them an email anytime, I always try to find a solution to whatever problem or question I have before I approach them. I do seek my mentors' advice though.

Mentors let you borrow someone else's knowledge.

You can try to navigate business or corporate life without one, but you'll end up making way more mistakes and bad decisions than you need to. Mentors can give you advice and teach you the 'tricks of the trade' that no university course can teach you. Their real life experience is invaluable. Over the years, I've sought out mentors who were living my dream. That's how I came across YouTube influencer and sexologist, Shannon Boodram who helped me through writing my book; fashion and lifestyle blogger, Shannae Ingleton who helped me land my first job as a journalist; therapist and tech founder, Bea Arthur, who taught me how to leverage my resources and turn a test into a testimony; Rakia Reynolds, a PR queen and founder of Skai Blue Media who hired me on as a staff writer for her company; motivational speaker Stuart Knight, who has advised me throughout my speaking career; and Charreah Jackson, the Love and Relationships Editor at Essence who taught me to be specific with my requests and not be afraid to ask for more, both to God and in business deals. Without these amazing people, I don't know how long it would have taken me to learn the lessons I did or access the opportunities they gave me. When I say mentorship is key, I mean it.

If you don't have a mentor, it's about time you start working towards that kind of relationship. But how do you find a mentor and how do you know who to choose. I have six qualities that are essential to good mentorship.

1. Experience

Nisha Moodley says, "Masters learn from masters." Mentorship is about learning from someone who's achieved the things you want. There's no sense in learning from someone who isn't qualified to give you advice.

2. Honesty

If you wanted to know the sunny side of a career, all you have to do is scroll Instagram. You need a mentor who's going to be real with you about the struggles and challenges because they'll understand how to help you turn your underdog past into a successful future.

3. Ambition

There is no point in approaching a mentor who is living a life of mediocrity. You need someone who is a dreamer, believer, doer and thinker, a professional risk-taker. If they're ambitious, they're going to push you too.

4. Vibes on the same frequency

Mentorship isn't just a business exchange. It's a partnership, a relationship. If your energy levels aren't on par, the relationship is going to feel forced. If it feels forced, move on. It doesn't mean they're a bad mentor. It just means they aren't meant to be yours.

5. Agrees to create structure around your relationship

You should take the initiative to suggest a schedule that's beneficial to both of you, whether that's an hour once a month, or 30 minutes once a week. Take initiative and be specific about how much time you require of your mentor and establish whether or not this will be a short- or long-term relationship. The reality is some people will be in your life for a reason and season, not necessarily a lifetime.

6. Thinks differently than you

You don't need to be in an echo chamber. If a mentor is feeding you information you already know, you're not learning anything. A good mentor is an out-of-the-box thinker that will challenge your beliefs and push you to your limits.

With these six qualities, you'll have a mentorship relationship that you'll constantly learn from and will also encourage you to do more and take more chances, knowing you have support and advice to back you up. Again, remember your mentor is not a substitute for Google or seeking your own answers, but they are an invaluable source of wisdom and advice when you need extra guidance. Get a good mentor in your corner, and I promise, it'll change the game for you.

Chapter 4:
So, What Now?

HIT THE BOOKS

Pauleanna

Now that you've decided to get clear on your vision, you need to be extremely selective about what you feed your mind. Endless scrolling through social media and Netflix binge sessions may be fun or whatever, but they aren't going to give you any kind of direction. My advice? Put your phone down, turn the TV off, and head out to a bookstore. (Or fire up Amazon. E-books are dope too.)

When I was first figuring out what to do with my life, I spent a lot of time reading: memoirs and biographies on entrepreneurs and public figures who inspired me; books about business and branding; self-help books that helped me ditch bad habits and shift my mindset, business and lifestyle magazines packed with profiles of amazing people. I may not have been able to sit down and speak with people I aspired to be like, but reading their thoughts, experiences, and advice was the next best thing. I buried myself in the pages of their books and applied their lessons and practices to my life where I could.

At every stage of your life, the mission should be to learn from people who have been where you are and who are living the lives you want. But especially now, when you're trying to find your footing and figure out what to do with your life, it's extremely important to be learning as much as you can.

Of course, the library you build will evolve as you get clearer on your purpose, but there are some amazing reads I've found super helpful that I think would be useful to just about anybody.

Read Shoe Dog by Phil Knight to see just how messy the path to success can be.

I first picked up Shoe Dog because it kept popping up everywhere. I saw it on the Lit Squad Instagram account and made a mental note to grab a copy. But then a few weeks later, I had three different people call me and tell me that I needed to read it. So, I went out and bought myself a copy. It was honestly so dope, but what else would you expect from the memoir of the man who created one of the most successful sneaker brands ever. Phil Knight's story of how he became the founder of Nike is insane and full of lessons I think everyone should learn.

In one of my favorite quotes from the book, he talks about how he had to determine his own definition of success.

"Like all my friends, I wanted to be successful. Unlike my friends, I didn't know what that meant. Money? Maybe. Wife? Kids? House? Sure, if I was lucky. These were the goals I was taught to aspire to, and part of me did aspire to them, instinctively. But deep down, I was searching for something else, something more. I had an aching sense that our time is short, shorter than we ever know, short as a morning run, and I wanted mine to be meaningful. And purposeful. And creative. And important. Above all...different. I wanted to leave a mark on the world. I wanted to win."

Damn, right? That's a word. And this is just a taste of how good this book is. Phil Knight's story is definitely a must-read if you're feeling unsure of your direction.

Read E-Squared by Pam Grout to get your attitude towards life right.

I'm a total believer in the law of attraction. Even if life is at its worst, your attitude matters. You don't want to ruin what may be in store for you because you let your negative mindset get in the way. The law of attraction is very real. E-Squared is an easy and interesting read for people who are struggling to maintain an attitude of positivity.

Here's a dope quote:

"Scarcity and lack is our default setting, the unquestioned condition that defines our lives. The belief that 'there's not enough' starts first thing every morning when the alarm clock rings: 'Ah shit, I didn't get through enough Z's.' Before we even sit up, before we even squeeze our feet into our bunny slippers, we're already bemoaning lack. When we finally do get up, it's 'Now I don't have enough time to get ready.' And from there it goes downhill. We spend large chunks of our energy worrying and complaining about not getting enough. We don't have enough time. We don't get enough exercise or fiber or vitamin E. Our paychecks aren't big enough. Our weekends aren't long enough. It never occurs to us to examine whether this 'not enough' mantra is true."

This is so real. And if it's something you're having a hard time with, Pam Grout doesn't play around about helping you ditch that 'not enough' narrative with the quickness. This is definitely a dope read if you need a perspective shift.

Read Tools of Titans by Tim Ferriss for advice from some of the best minds in the game.

This is by far one of the best books I've read in a long time. I can't tell you how much the tactics, routines, and habits I learned from this book have enriched my life. There's something so fascinating about the way successful people think and do things. One of my favorite pieces of advice is from Seth Godin: "[The First Ten] is a simple theory of marketing that says: tell ten people, show ten people, share it with ten people; ten people who already trust you and like you. If they don't tell anyone else, it's not that good, and you should start over. If they do tell other people, then you're on your way." Tools of Titans is full of simple but practical advice like this that are helpful if you're starting a business, or even just considering the idea. If the goal is to become wildly successful, then you need to make this one of your manuals.

Read Platform by Michael Hyatt for the best tips on how to get people to hear you.

This is one of the resources that helped me get my brand off the ground. Michael Hyatt is a straight-shooter. His advice is practical and very easy to understand. I've read this book four times and found applicable tips for the stage I'm at with every read. It's my go-to for any questions around social media, building a tribe and "wrapping WOW in style" (which is my favorite chapter, by the way). Even if you're not 100% sure what your goals are, this book is a solid foundation on how to "get noticed in a noisy world."

There were points in the journey when I was really discouraged, and I remember this quote stood out to me: "You will never see the full path. The important thing is to do the next right thing. What can you do today to move you toward your dream?" But Hyatt doesn't just leave you to sit and struggle to find the answer to that question. He provides tons of advice and direction to help you figure out what that next right thing might be. That's why this book should definitely be in your library.

These are just four of probably a hundred amazing books I've read. Over the years, I've picked up books that were perfect for the stage I was at because they addressed the questions and challenges I was dealing with at the time. Others were really relevant to my business and industry. These four I've suggested are a great start for pretty much anyone, but always be on the lookout for other reads that can help you along your way.

Andrew

I used to read a ton when I started out. Whenever I had spare time, I was deep in a book. I realized that I was a young twenty-something and no matter how much life had already taught me, there was way more that I didn't know. That's the funny thing about knowledge — we can't even begin to imagine how little we actually know because we only know what we've seen personally. But successful people know that they can get an edge by tapping into other people's experiences and learning from their mistakes, lessons, and advice. Reading gives you a chance to do that. So, why wouldn't you take it?

Don't tell me you don't have time to read. You're not making time. Even if you only get 15 minutes to read every day, that's 15 more minutes worth of knowledge you didn't have before. Pick up a book and read it on your way to work or class. Scan a book when you sit down to eat — you only need one hand to hold a fork, right? E-books make it easy for you to read just about anywhere. Download them on your phone and read those while you're waiting for an appointment instead of scrolling through social media. If you have trouble focusing on reading, grab the audio version of the book. There are apps for that. But make it happen. Consider it an investment. You give your time and a few bucks, and you get a whole lot of knowledge in return that can help you start a business, boost your career, or improve yourself. I'd say that's a worthwhile trade.

Just like Pauleanna, I've built a library of my own. It's been a while since I've read some of these books, but I still remember a lot of the lessons I learned from them. That's why I think you should read them too.

Read The 48 Laws of Power by Robert Greene to learn how to get control of your life.

There's a reason this book is a best-seller. Robert Greene went in! He uses 48 laws to give great insights you can apply to live a life full of optimism and progress. He makes reference to hundreds of powerful figures over the past 3000 years, so you're not just learning from the author, but some of the most influential people to ever live. You need to read this because we can't pretend that understanding and having power isn't important. Power is what lets you dominate as an entrepreneur. It helps you negotiate job positions, salaries, and benefits. It helps you navigate relationships with people above you. Especially at a point in your life when you're trying to figure out what you want, understanding how to be in control is an important first step.

One of my favorite laws is "Re-create yourself." Greene says, "Do not accept the roles that society foists on you. Re-create yourself by forging a new identity, one that commands attention and never bores the audience. Be the master of your own image rather than letting others define it for you." As someone who helps people build and strengthen their brands, I love that rule.

When you read the book, different laws are going to stand out to you depending on what you're going through or what's important in your life right now. But there's something in there for everybody.

Read The Compound Effect by Darren Hardy to learn how to grow what you have.

One of the things I tell anyone who comes to me for advice is to think long-term. If you're making decisions now without thinking about what it's going to mean in the future, you're just screwing yourself. That's why I really recommend reading The Compound Effect. Darren Hardy uses the principle of investing and applies them to life. He helps you see how every decision you make impacts your life and gives you the keys to taking small steps that will have the big outcomes you want.

Here's a dope quote:

"Forget about willpower. It's time for why-power. Your choices are only meaningful when you connect them to your desires and dreams. The wisest and most motivating choices are the ones aligned with that which you identify as your purpose, your core self, and your highest values. You've got to want something, and know why you want it, or you'll end up giving up too easily."

If you've been struggling to make good decisions and can't figure out how to get what you want no matter how hard you're trying, read The

Compound Effect and get you some "why-power."

Read How to Win Friends and Influence People by Dale Carnegie to...well, learn how to win friends and influence people.

The title says it all. This book is like the go-to guide for learning how to build relationships and make them work for you. But it might not be what you expect. I realize that this generation has grown up really self-absorbed. A lot of us are coddled by our parents, and we live our whole lives focused on what makes us happy. How to Win Friends and Influence People flips the script because it's not about entitlement and receiving. It's about giving to get the results you want. Dale Carnegie gives the rules for how to connect with people, influence them, and get a leg up when you need things like support, mentorship, or sponsorship.

Let me give you a little sample. One of the things Dale Carnegie talks about is learning to ditch self-centeredness in conversations. He says, "Why talk about what we want? That is childish. Absurd. Of course, you are interested in what you want. You are eternally interested in it. But no one else is. The rest of us are just like you: we are interested in what we want."

How to Win Friends and Influence People is full of nuggets like that to help you build relationships that actually matter and make them work for you.

Read The E-Myth: Revisited by Michael Gerber to figure out if you're really crazy enough to be an entrepreneur.

Being an entrepreneur isn't for everybody. If you're considering entrepreneurship, but you're not really sure, you need to grab a copy of *The E-Myth: Revisited*. Because, the fact is you need to be a certain type of person to be a successful entrepreneur. This book looks at why businesses fail and what it takes to succeed. And if you decide that you are built for entrepreneurship, and you want to jump in, the book will also give you tips and advice on how to approach your business to make sure you don't screw yourself.

There's a lot you can take away from this book. For example, Gerber says, "I believe it's true that the difference between great people and everyone else is that great people create their lives actively, while everyone else is created by their lives, passively waiting to see where life takes them next."

So, what do you want: to be great or to be everyone else? You better say be great, and then get to reading.

These are my top four right now, but here are some honorable mentions. The Alchemist is great for discovering your purpose and defining yourself. The 4 Hour Work Week will help you think smart, be productive, and use the internet to get what you want. And The 10X Rule will show you how to put in the amount of effort it really takes to succeed. Start with the books Pauleanna and I recommended, but don't let that be the end. Keep reading and expanding your knowledge so that when the time comes to apply it, you're ready.

PASSION, PURPOSE, AND THE THINGS IN BETWEEN

························ ⊙⊰⊱⊙ ························

Andrew

I hate the word passion. You may be thinking, "Why?! Isn't passion the thing that makes entrepreneurs tick." It absolutely is. Most successful people I know are super passionate about their businesses or careers. But that kind of passion is rare, and that's why I hate the word—because most people don't know what it really means. What I should say is that I hate the way most people use the word passion. It's become one of those overused words like "love." People are just tossing it around without understanding that it's something really deep.

Most people hear the word passion, and they start thinking about something they really love. Ask most people what they're passionate about, and they'll tell you about the hobby they do on the weekends, or that thing they've been interested in for a couple of years. It's usually something pretty surface level, things that entertain them or make them temporarily happy.

But passion is so much more than that. It's the thing that gets you out of bed in the morning and makes you want to hit the ground running. Passion is what helps you pry your eyes open and read industry magazines when all you want to do is sleep. Passion isn't just about liking something. It's about being obsessed with it, being willing to grind day in and day out and do whatever it takes to make that thing you love a reality.

Let's be real. A lot of us think we're passionate about something until it gets hard. How many people do you know that were crazy passionate about playing ball until they came up on some kids that were bigger and faster than them on the court? Suddenly, they weren't dreaming of the NBA anymore. Or the artist who quits sending in demos to recording studios after the second or third rejection and decides music isn't really their thing. Some people change their "passions" all the time because they're looking for something that's going to feel easy and fun forever.

But real passion isn't just about this idea that we can do what we love for the rest of our lives or that we're going to be happily living our dreams. Of course, that's the goal, but life isn't perfect, and success definitely isn't that simple. Withstanding the challenges, failure, rejection, exhaustion and everything else that makes other people quit takes passion. When you're really passionate about something, it's because it's the thing that fulfills you, the thing that gives you purpose, and nothing can make you quit that.

Find your purpose, and you'll really discover passion.

Whenever I meet young aspiring entrepreneurs, and they start talking about their "passions," I always ask them to think instead about the thing that makes them feel fulfilled—that's purpose. I want them to discover the thing that they'd be willing to do for the next five, ten, or even twenty years. Because that's the kind of long-haul you're in for. Everybody imagines the end goal, the big moment of success, but they don't realize that it's years and years to get to that point. If it's something that truly fulfills you and gives you purpose, it'll be possible to stay passionate through all the years of hard work. That sense of purpose makes it possible for you to love the process even when it's uncomfortable. But if you're just doing the thing that caught your interest most recently, that "passion" is going to wear off real fast, and you'll be quitting at the first signs of struggle.

Finding your purpose takes a lot of looking inward. And it definitely isn't easy. To figure out what it is that's going to make you tick for the next few decades, you have to spend some time really thinking about what you do best. I like how my friend Kevin Matthew explains it "You have to figure out exactly what it is that you really want and know what it is going to cost in terms of time and difficulty. You have to ask around [to find out the costs] and be realistic with yourself. But even though you can start a business and do all this great stuff and go into consulting or whatever it is, it's still going to be difficult. Even though that's your purpose and your calling, it doesn't make it easy."

Purpose is about your unique offering to the world—the thing that you do well and care about that can change other people's lives.

Follow your gifts and talents, not the fads.

It's easy for people to get caught up in what's hot at the moment and think it's their passion because they see people succeeding off of it. That's why we have hundreds of "social media entrepreneurs" popping up on IG claiming they can teach you how to live a jet-set lifestyle. Everywhere you look, there are life coaches and personal brand strategists who really aren't equipped but are following the latest fad because that's what's popping right now. Every few years, a new thing becomes popular, and suddenly, it's everybody's passion.

That doesn't mean there aren't people excelling at those things. But when it comes to things like that, the real get separated out from the bandwagoners fast because if you lack the actual skills and dedication to pull it off, you're going to fail. So the question is, are you sure that's your passion? If you answer confidently, that's great, do it. If you hesitate, you've already lost. Either way, it's still going to be hard, and either way, your response doesn't matter to me or the market. Once you've developed and built upon your passion is when we know it's real.

If you're trying to figure out what you're meant to do, stop spending so much time scrolling your timelines and follow your natural gifts and talents. Your purpose can't be based on what everybody else does well because you're not everybody else. There's no sense in you throwing yourself into something trendy that you're no good at just because it's making someone else successful. That trendy thing is making them successful because they're good at it, and they've found a way to make it useful to other people. Take your talents and gifts, practice and strengthen them, and then figure out how you can use them to make other people's lives better.

Alex Wolf, the founder of Boss Babe Inc., is an amazing example of this. She started using computers when she was just two years old, and she's always had a love for the Internet. Back in 2013, when businesses hadn't really picked up on the value of social media yet, she started doing consultations to help brands build their social media presence. In the meantime, she noticed that all the empowerment for entrepreneurs on Instagram was about men. Ferraris and lions and motivational quotes about being a man in business were everywhere, but there was nothing targeted at women. So, she took her knack for social media and straight talking and started creating motivational posts for women in business. Women loved it, and now Boss Babe is one of the biggest platforms and communities for female entrepreneurs.

I have so much respect for how Alex took something that she's been good at all her life and made it into something so amazing. But that's what happens when you're truly passionate about something that gives you purpose.

I swear finding your purpose and living in it just completely changes the way you even look at life. I can honestly say that I'm not afraid to die because I'm living in my purpose. Don't believe me? Let me tell you a little story.

In January 2016, I got robbed at gunpoint. It's one of those things that seems unreal. But I got in my car, and there was this guy less than two feet from me with a gun pointed dead in my face. Nothing really prepares you for that, and it's hard to know how you'd react until it's happening. But it's like some instinct kicked in, and I decided to fight back. I grabbed the nozzle of the gun and started wrestling with this guy. He fights back a bit, grabs some stuff, and runs off.

My first thought was like, "Alright, cool. I'm good. Time to get back to work." I wasn't even going to call the police because I wasn't interested in spending hours talking to officers and doing paperwork. My brain was right back in work mode. But I decided to call the police and file a report so that maybe they could catch this guy and keep him from sticking up anybody else. Before the ink was dry on that report, I was back home and working.

But if you thought this story was insane before, it gets wilder. The next day, I got in my car, and something told me to look in the backseat. I guess that robber wasn't too passionate about his life of crime because he'd left his wallet with all his ID in my backseat. And then, not even a few hours later, I went into the back of my car for something, and when I opened the door, out fell a loaded 9mm gun. Look at God! I turned everything in, the guy got caught, and I spent six months involved in the court case. When it was finally over, I was glad he got caught, but my biggest relief was that I could get back to fully focusing on my business. It's not that I don't recognize the severity of the situation. I definitely realize I could have died that night, just a few days after my 26th birthday. But it didn't freak me out that much simply because I'm not afraid to die. And I'm not afraid to die because I'm confident that I'm living my life in my purpose.

I am so fulfilled by what I do, and I'm going to do this till I draw my last breath. I know it's a huge blessing to be in a position to have a business that I'm so passionate about. If you're not there yet, don't sit back and sweat, start working. Find what gives you purpose and be ready to die for it. Because once you get to that point, you will truly be living.

Pauleanna

Just like Andrew, I'm living in my purpose, and nothing else makes me feel more fulfilled. I run three businesses and manage 22 freelancers. I'm full-time tired, but I feel fulfilled every single day. I'm rich, bruh, and I don't mean money rich. Yeah, I'm doing well, but I don't do this for the money. I don't live this life for the cash. I chase my dreams because I believe that when you focus on your passion and master it, all the pleasures that come with having a successful business follow naturally.

For me, the goal has always been happiness. And like Andrew said, following your passion doesn't mean you're going to be happy all the time. Nah, far from it. But the point is, anyone can take their passion and turn a profit if they're willing to focus and put in the work. But the passion is key. If you're not passionate about what you're doing, you're just wasting time. If you want to be successful, whatever you choose to pursue has to align with your beliefs and values.

The reason I dropped out of my college program was that the thought of doing business admin for the rest of my life made me want to scream. I'm willing to bet that if I had stuck it out in that degree, I would have ditched it at some point anyway. I was just meant to be doing something else, and I knew it. You have to find out what drives you because you will not succeed unless you have a purpose for why you do what you do.

One of my early mentors and close friends, Shannon Boodram, is a great example. At 18, she was at college on a track and field scholarship. In the middle of a meet, someone asked her why she was always so cranky before races, and it dawned on her that she was miserable because she hated the sport. She just didn't feel passionate about it. She moved back home to Canada and went to school for journalism, and it lit up her life. Her rap sheet includes articles in national newspapers, celebrity interviews, hosting a television sports show, interning at MTV, and publishing a sex-education book. If you follow Shannon on Instagram, you know she's living her best life as a sexologist and author. She's got a wildly popular YouTube channel, been featured on The View, and is hosting a talk show on Facebook. Her life is proof that when you follow your passion, it pays off.

But Andrew's right. A lot of people have no idea what passion really means or what their true purpose is, and they definitely need to take some time to seek that out. Because purpose is the thing that steers you through your goals. That realization really hit me when I first started writing my novel, Everything I Couldn't Tell My Mother in 2008. It had been one of my goals for a long time, and with some encouragement and a push in the right direction from a few friends, I created a chapter-by-chapter summary and set out on this new journey. But I kept getting stuck. I couldn't get past my writer's block until I stopped and identified what was most important to me and cut out everything else. I got rid of all the distractions that were stunting my writing. I immersed myself in writing that novel, spending hours every day creating my story. Yes, it took me four years, and I had to push through a whole lot of challenges, but because I had taken the time to define my purpose, it guided me through the process, and I was finally able to write the novel I'd always dreamed of. Like Andrew said, find your purpose, and you'll really discover passion and everything you need to fulfill it. If you're still not sure of your purpose, commit to figuring it out.

But I want to talk to the people on the other end of the spectrum — those people who know their purpose and are just sitting down on it. Look, I'm not trying to judge you because I've been you. I've always been a big dreamer, but I didn't always have the courage to go after those dreams. I let fear slow me down and other people's opinions discourage me. When my high school teachers told me I couldn't be a writer, I doubted myself. And then I sat down in college lecture halls for two whole years listening to professors drone on about things I didn't care about instead of going after my passion.

But there comes a point when I had to realize that nobody was going to take my hand and guide me to my purpose. I had been letting people hold my hand and guide my steps all through high school and college and look where that got me. No, if I wanted to fulfill my purpose and live in my passion, I had to start making moves.

If you know your purpose, get moving.

You've got to stop sitting on your passion. Seriously, get up off your butt and put in the work. I know, I know, you're talented. But talent isn't enough. It never is. Because there are about a thousand people with your talent working in the same spaces and for the same opportunities as you. The only way you're going to secure your success is if you start matching that talent with some regular ass hard work.

And I do mean work. You can't win if you don't play, and you can't play well unless you practice. When I was in high school, the only class I excelled in was gym because I was a natural athlete. Math, Science, English—none of that came naturally to me. But athletics, I had that on lock. Doesn't mean I didn't practice though. When I said I was a high-performance athlete, I meant it.

Growing up, I was a champion competitive swimmer with my eyes on the Olympics. Every morning, for ten years, I was in the pool at 5:00 swimming laps. Then after school, I spent an hour lifting weights, and another two hours in the pool. There were mornings when my shoulders burned, and my legs ached, but I still showed up and swam those laps. It was that insane dedication that allowed me to travel across the country and win national level swim meets. Sure, I was a naturally good swimmer, but it was the practice that set me apart from the competition.

When I finally decided that I wanted to pursue my passion for writing, speaking, and mentorship, I dived in with the same dedication. I read and wrote every single day, morning and evening, just like those swim practices. I knew if I wanted to be in the arena with successful journalists, authors, and speakers, I needed to give my talent a boost by always striving to be the best.

Don't ever make the mistake of thinking talent is enough.

I don't care how good you are at something. It's not enough. It's never enough. No shade, but there are about a thousand people who are as good as you and a thousand more who are better. And then there are the thousands who aren't as talented as you are, but they work harder. You know what's going to help you stand out amongst them? Building on that talent. You can't expect to be great if you want to skate by on your talents or only grind sometimes. Winning at anything means grinding every single day.

If this sounds challenging, that's because it is. That whole thing about "if you do what you love, you'll never work a day in your life" is crap. When you figure out your passion and start pursuing it, you're going to have to work harder than ever. But passion is like fuel. If you're really passionate about something, you'll find the energy to work a 9-to-5 and then go home and spend hours reading about the biggest players in your field or practicing your craft. You'll be willing to sacrifice chill time, family time, and turn up time, to put in the hours it takes to become great.

Chapter 5:
Augmented Reality

BRAND AROUND YOU

Pauleanna

I have a funny relationship with social media. It's one of my biggest assets, but that's because of the way I approach it. A lot of people allow social media to distract them, scrolling through their phones when they could be doing something else. Or they get caught up in other people's highlight reels and get discouraged with their own progress. But for me, I work carefully to make sure social media isn't a distraction or discouragement. It's a tool. Even when I didn't know much of anything and hardly had any experience, my social media attracted mentors and great opportunities.

Even if you're still in the process of deciding what you want, you need to be careful to make your social media work for you. That means being mindful of the kinds of things you tweet and the photos you post. Pictures of you getting drunk every weekend? Not a good look. Rude and offensive tweets? You might not want to do that.

It's not a joke when they say the internet is forever. It really is. Even those things you tweet and delete don't necessarily disappear. And while you may not care now, in a year, or five, or ten, when you have people deciding if they want to work with you, sloppy, untasteful social media behaviors might come back to bite you in the ass.

Even if you develop an impeccable offline reputation, your online persona matters too. Before you even walk into an interview, employers will Google you and snoop through snapshots of your life on all social media networks. If you start a business, before a client purchases a product/service, they want to know if you're trustworthy, what you represent, and what you stand for. Bottom line, your first impression can make or break you. You simply don't know who is watching and what power they hold, so my primary advice is always to put your best foot forward.

Make sure your social is immaculate by Googling yourself.

Hit up that search bar, type in your name, and see what pops up. This will help you get an idea of what your reputation looks like right now. Stalk your Facebook posts, tweets, YouTube channel, and Instagram pics. If you think your character looks great and you're comfortable with what you present, dope. Go a step further and have a friend give you a second opinion. Make sure it's someone who will be honest with you instead of feeding you the lies they think you want to hear.

Don't think you have to fake it though.

The point isn't to present some sort of false image. You want your social media to showcase your strengths and interests. It's not about being some boring representation of what employers want. Feel free to post pictures of your hobbies and friends. Share your thoughts on Facebook posts and tweets. You can be real and genuine. What you want to stay away from is things that look tacky or that are flat out offensive, especially if that's not the kind of image you want to present. If you find something that doesn't sit right, delete it.

Instead, show off a little bit...or a lot.

Your social media is your platform to shine. Like a resume, almost. So, don't be shy to show off and show out a little bit. If you're well traveled, drop those cool vacation photos on the 'gram. If you're a fashion junkie, snap your favorite outfits. Tweet about books or magazines that you're reading. Share your cool experiences or dope opportunities you're exploring. All of those are things people have literally built brands off of. Think fashion bloggers, IG travel accounts, YouTube book reviewers. It may not be a main gig, but you never know if those things could turn into side hustles or job opportunities. So, let yourself shine.

Books shouldn't be judged by their cover, but they usually are, so make that profile picture pop.

I find fuzzy profile pics so irritating. If the first thing I see when I get on your profile is a pixelated low-quality picture of you, I question how you handle other parts of your life. It seems trivial, but it's a bit like getting up and leaving the house without washing your face. If you can't manage to make an effort with your presentation, it makes me question if other things are sloppy too. I'm not saying to go out and hire a professional photographer for headshots if you can't afford one—although if you can, you should. But if you've got a smartphone with a decent camera, find a white wall, wear a nice shirt, comb your hair, and get someone to take a clear, focused, flattering headshot of you until you can get a photographer to hook you up with a professional shot.

Be careful of the things you think other people can't see.

Your timeline may be flawless and professional, but remember that your likes on Twitter and Facebook and playlists on YouTube are publicly visible too. Earlier this year, political candidate Ted Cruz took some serious heat for liking a questionable tweet on Twitter. It was tucked away in his favorites, but that didn't mean no one could see it. So while you're watching the face you put forward, mind the things you do behind the scenes too.

Take notes from the greats.

Whether you have a brand figured out or not, it's always a good idea to look at people who have branded themselves in ways you admire and take notes. For me, I follow the brands of Alex Elle, Marie Forleo, Ashley Chea , Vashtie Kola, Angela Rye, Karen Civil, and other polished but straight-talking women with killer style. They match up with who I want to be and how I want to be seen and checking out their brands helps me nail down my own.

Whatever you do, remember that your social media is a personal branding tool and one of a few spaces where you have total control of the narrative. It's in your best interest to re-evaluate your online presence so that you can open up a window filled with new opportunities. If you have a business idea, want to switch careers, want to make a profit from your true passion, or you're still just figuring it out, creating a strong personal brand can help you achieve all of that.

Andrew

I know a lot of business gurus and millennial experts are obsessed with social media and push it like some sort of magic pill for success, but I'm not in that camp. I legit think that social media isn't the end all and be all some people make it out to be, especially from a personal branding standpoint. I personally believe that social media is more of an asset to people who already have successful businesses because it's an amazing marketing tool. But it's easy for individuals to get caught up and lost in the sauce.

But I'm not going to deny that, when you use it right, social media can definitely be a beneficial tool for people trying to get a leg up. Like Pauleanna said, social media is a space that lets you establish the narrative online in front of thousands instead of just the people you meet face-to-face. It lets you take who you are in real life and represent it according to what you want to be known for. But to really nail it, you need to build something that attracts the people you want, and that starts with figuring out what story you're really trying to tell.

People can't believe in something you don't even understand yourself.

On social media, you tell the story, and people either buy into it, or they don't. But I guarantee no one is going to be on board with the story you push on social media if you don't even know it yourself. I see so many people trying to be motivators and talking a big game online, and I can smell the fake a mile away. I can tell they're just spitting back things they read somewhere that sounded good. But it's not true to them. You can't fake authenticity. People don't believe in anything that isn't genuine.

Gary Vee talks about documenting vs. creating. That's how you avoid the trap of being a reality star under a false narrative. Instead, you're speaking your authentic truth. Authenticity is one of the biggest reasons my personal brand has grown. I'm not flexin' for the 'gram. What looks like other people's flex is my real life. Some people bought a car and went into debt to look the part. I bought mine in cash because I worked until I reached a point where I could do that. See the difference? One is trying to be something, creating an image, while the other is actually being present and authentic.

So, don't try to be something, just be you. Figure out who you are, and then be that. That's not necessarily license to do whatever you want online though. At least not yet.

There are definitely "rules," but you're not going to find them in a manual.

As much as I'm encouraging you to do what's authentic to you, understand that in the social media game, there are still rules you have to play by. If you were on an island by yourself, you could do whatever you want without caring about the impact. Those drunken posts Pauleanna warned you about wouldn't matter at all. But you're sharing the world with other people, and you need to be cautious of that in your social media. When you post, take into account the political climate and hot-button topics. Sensitivity actually matters, and you should be practicing it. This is especially true if you're hoping social media will get you job opportunities.

There are levels to this. You gotta know if you're in a position to break the "rules."

Some people can say, do, and post anything they want online because they're not really counting on anyone for opportunities. They've built businesses of their own or developed a personal brand so dope and unique that people are just about dying to work with them. If you're not on that level, fall back a little. Realize that when you're starting from the bottom, you have to stay humble. You can't just post all cavalier when you know you're counting on someone to employ you. Know where you're at and play accordingly.

Know when it's time to customize your social for the things you want.

If you're trying to get your foot into certain doors, you need to cater your social media to help you with that goal. Say you're trying to become an influencer or get a job in a particular industry. You need to make your social media appeal to the people in those spaces. Yes, that means posting content that's attractive to them instead of all the things you wanted to post. Because when you're a newbie, you need to do what it takes to get noticed and realize that you don't have the leverage to ignore the interest of the people you want to attract. But think of it is a temporary sacrifice, a means to an end.

No matter your goal, though, say something worth listening to.

If you get on social media and everything you post is hot air and vanity, no one is going to care. You need to add value. And again, not those recycled motivational messages, but the value that is authentic to you. That means really committing to spending time offline learning where your value lies. It could be as simple as sharing about the things you're learning, letting people in on tips in your area of expertise, or being candid about your journey. But bring some sort of value to the world through your captions, stories, and images. People stick around if you're offering them something, no matter what stage you're at.

No matter how much of this advice you follow though, remember that social media can only get you so far. If you build some amazing online brand, but you're boring offline, you've just wasted your time. It's false advertising, and when people realize, they're out. Commit to creating a genuine personality and real value offline, and use social media to expand the reach of your real life work and accomplishments.

Chapter 6:
Undecided Doesn't Have to Mean Broke

FAST TRACK – GETTING ON THE FRANCHISE

Andrew

Starting a business from scratch is hard. I'm sure any entrepreneur will tell you that's true. Even when you think you've got everything figured out, you've done all the research, asked all the right questions, and put all the right things in place, something comes out of left field to test your resolve.

How bad do you really want this?

You better know. Because the challenges are going to come. So, for people who aren't 100% sure what they want to do, starting a business is intimidating and even more of a challenge. But that doesn't mean that people who want to be entrepreneurs but don't have a solid business idea should just sit on their hands and do nothing with that ambition. What if I told you there was a way to have your own business without going through all the startup strife?

A lot of you are probably thinking about multi-level marketing (or MLM). I just want to clear the air around this: I don't think it's a good business model. The market is oversaturated with people selling health products, leggings, and that sort of thing through MLM. I don't think there's a single person in North America who hasn't had an old friend hit them up for coffee or whatever, only to realize they were getting caught in an MLM pitch. I'm not denying that it works for some people, and it's great for learning sales skills, but I dislike it for two reasons: 1) you don't get to establish your own brand; and 2) it's all about the money and the transaction, and the human element that's so important to business just gets thrown out. The focus is just on sales and recruiting. Like Gary Vee says, if your plan is to grow your personal brand eventually, MLM is not the way to go. There's too much stigma, and once you get labeled a multi-level marketer, it's hard to shake that reputation, and it'll probably follow you into all your future endeavors. If that's your hustle, do you, but I just want to be real.

If you're looking for a better option, I would suggest going the route of the franchise. A franchise is when a business (franchisor) licenses its trade name and business system to an independent owner (franchisee), and the franchisee runs the business in line with the terms of the license. The simplest way to explain it: you buy an existing store and follow the rules of the business. There are a lot of well-known businesses that are franchises, including hotels like Ramada and Hampton; restaurants like Pita Pit, McDonald's, and Wendy's; and fitness chains like Snap Fitness and Anytime Fitness. Hundreds of businesses are franchises and have hundreds or thousands of locations across the US that are run by entrepreneurs.

The franchisors have to maintain brand standards like logos, uniforms, and products and services but are otherwise free to operate the business however they want within the license terms. I'll be real. Franchising isn't cheap. There are usually some hefty upfront costs, especially for big names like McDonald's and Chik-fil-A. But if you've got some extra cash in the bank, there are lesser-known more affordable franchises you can buy into for as low as $2,500.

Franchises have a lot of upsides. Because you're getting into an established business, you don't have to worry about what product you'll sell, what operation system to use, or who your client base is. That's already decided for you. And if a business is doing well enough to franchise, those products, systems, and client bases are usually pretty reliable. The franchisor provides you with tools and support to help you through running the business, so you're not left trying to figure out how to get started and keep things running. In many cases, they'll even help you set up the store, train your staff, and get in touch with reputable suppliers.

Of course, nothing is perfect. There are some cons to a franchise. Besides the fact that the initial start-up cost can be high, you may also have to pay royalties on your sales, making profits slow. If you're looking for an opportunity to develop your own brand, that's not really an option with franchises. You've bought into an established brand, and you have to maintain the standards their customers expect. If you want to change anything, you have to get approval from the franchisor first. You can't just mess with their brand without their permission. And there's also the risk of losing customers and profits if there's bad publicity for the brand.

I'm definitely not saying there aren't any risks, but if you play it right, the perks are real. I've seen entrepreneurs get really successful because of franchises. A friend of mine, a few years back, wanted to get into business but hadn't figured out what his passion was. So, he bought a franchise. He was able to learn the ropes of running a business without the risk of creating a startup he wasn't sure about. It was like business management 101, except he got to make a real profit. After a few years as a franchisee, he was able to figure out the business he really wanted to run, and with the info he learned from running the franchise, he was able to build his own business that's now worth a quarter million dollars.

If franchising sounds like it could work for you, here are a few with lower startup costs that are worth considering:

1. Chester's Chicken

The popular fried chicken chain has licenses for as low as $8,639. They've also got an established customer base that already knows and loves the brand. If you've got a retail space available, they can have you operating in a few weeks, and they provide in-store training for staff.

2. Proforma

Proforma provides large corporations and mid-sized businesses with forms, promotional products, business documents, printing, and other services for advertising and business needs. Their initial investment can be as low as $4,730.

3. Buildingstars

This commercial cleaning service has been around for 17 years providing green cleaning and consulting, nightly cleaning, and carpet and floor care. You can get a franchise license with Buildingstars for as little as $2,245.

If you do decide to become a franchisee, just remember that, like any business, it's going to take hard work. Don't do it for the glamour or the ease, because it isn't either one of those things. It's a business that's going to take your dedication, focus, and energy. Whether you succeed or fail is still up to you, no matter how great of a business the franchise is. This isn't a golden ticket to entrepreneurial success. It's business. Make sure that before you put thousands of dollars into buying a franchise that you're ready to work your butt off to turn that investment into a profit.

NOTES

BRANDING FOR CORPORATE 9-5ERS

Chapter 7:
Top Floor, Corner Office

STARTED FROM THE BOTTOM

Pauleanna

If you Google the terms "9-to-5" and "hustle" together, pretty much every result talks about juggling a side hustle and corporate job, turning your side-hustle into a 9-to-5, or escaping your day job. Out of 460,000 results, almost none of them talk about the hustle it takes to be excellent at your 9-5. There's this misconception that if you're not building your own business, you're not really grinding. I want to kill that idea right now.

As Kate White says, "Career breakthroughs occur at the intersection of readiness, opportunity, and hustle."

Hustle?

Yes, hustle isn't just for entrepreneurs and brand builders. It's for you in your entry-level corporate gig too.

There's a lot of success to be had in corporate. If you want it, you have to be ready to put in work. A lot of CEOs, executives, and high-level employees at some of the world's biggest companies started out in entry-level positions. They got to where they were because they understood that climbing the corporate ladder is exactly that, a climb. You don't get anywhere if you want to sit on the bottom rung and chill. If you're going to succeed, you have to do what it takes to impress the people who matter.

I've worked in the corporate world for about as long as I've been an entrepreneur. When I walked out of my college exam all those years ago, it wasn't like I got my business up and running straight away. I still had to pay my bills, and I had mad debt. Not making money wasn't an option. I was twenty-something, broke as a joke, and barely qualified for anything. So, I found an entry-level job as a receptionist. There was nothing glamorous about it at all. But I showed up, worked hard, and made sure my boss never had a reason to fire me.

Around the time that I was working the receptionist job, my mentor, Shannae, got me the journalism gig with Mediaplanet Publishing House Canada Inc. I suddenly had two full-time entry-level corporate positions. As a new writer at a major journalism outlet, I kicked into a whole new gear of hustle. Because when you're the new girl on the block, you have everything to prove and no room to be anything less than the best.

Mediaplanet Canada is a content giant with an amazing reputation. I joined as a new writer whose only experience was writing on my blog. Bruh, my early days at that job were full of anxiety. Unlike my receptionist job, this one had no set hours, I worked remotely, and there wasn't a whole lot of supervision. And that made it even more nerve-wracking. It felt like there were a million more ways to mess up. I wasn't really sure what the hell I was doing, and I was terrified of disappointing Shannae. I remember getting my first assignment to write an article about holiday décor for the National Post. It was the first time I ever needed to interview anyone. I did my research, pulled off the interview, and produced the article on time. The article was published for hundreds of thousands of people to read. It was like experiencing a high. But I didn't allow that to go to my head. One article didn't mean I had arrived.

I was just getting started. Over the four years I worked with Mediaplanet Canada, I took on every assignment they offered me. Things other writers would say, "Hell no!" to, I took without a single complaint. That's how I got the chance to interview famed actress and singer Olivia Newton-John about her experience surviving breast cancer. She was halfway across the world, and the only time she would be available to interview was 3:00 am Eastern Standard Time. The finished article was due at 8:00 that same morning. I'm not surprised other people said no. But I knew saying yes didn't just mean a golden opportunity to put something great on my resume. It would make me a standout journalist. So, I said yes, and I made it happen. I got up the morning before, worked a full day, and then came home and stayed awake until it was time for the call because I didn't want to risk missing my alarm. I delivered the article, and it was published in the Toronto Star weeks later.

That was the level of determination I brought to that job every single day. I pulled all-nighters. I went into the office where I worked as a receptionist at 6:00 am just to finish articles. I booked boardrooms when I needed to do interviews during the day. I even hired a French tutor after my editor sent out an email seeking French writers. My tutor, Alison, came to my house every week for a year to teach me how to read and write in French. I never ended up fluent enough to write articles, but my editor was impressed that I was willing to go so far.

Always be prepared to do the most.

That's what it takes. Whatever entry-level job you're in, you have to be ready to be extra and always bring your A-game. Never half-ass anything. You have to treat every task like your entire career depends on it. That means doing more than the bare minimum. Way too often, people get caught up in the job description and figure that since that's what they get paid for that's all they're going to do. That attitude will keep you stuck on entry-level your whole career. Sure, it keeps your paycheck coming, but that's all you'll ever get.

Raises, promotions, and new opportunities don't get handed to the employee who just does what they're supposed to. Those privileges go to the people who will do what they're supposed to and then take it a step further. So, if your manager has given you an assignment, think about how you can expand on the task and kick it up a notch. Taking initiative is what impresses bosses and keeps you on the front of their mind when golden opportunities arise.

Say yes now, so you can hear yes in the future.

But don't just wait for those golden opportunities to say yes. Raise your hand whenever you get the chance, even if it costs you sleep and time. And even if it's boring as hell. Let's be real: entry-level roles are hardly ever brimming with exciting opportunities. A lot of the things you're asked to do are boring. Do them anyway. Those sacrifices you make now will pay off in the future. Just like taking initiative makes you stand out, so does a willingness to show up and say yes. When better opportunities come up, or you need to ask your boss for a raise or time off, you're way more likely to get the "yes."

But be patient with the process.

None of this happens overnight. It's a long haul going from entry-level to the top floor. There are going to be times you say yes, and it feels like you get nothing more out of it than hard work. Sometimes you'll be extra as hell and give your best on the task, and you'll barely get any recognition. You'll pull all-nighters, work late, come in early, raise your hand, and do everything, and it'll seem nothing is coming out of it. Stay patient and stay on it because every single step is necessary. Remember that success is a long haul no matter what you're doing. And the journey is important because it's where you build your character, your reputation, and your backbone.

Stay ready so you don't have to get ready.

Don't use patience as an excuse for laziness, though. If all you do is wait, all you'll get is nothing. Use the hours outside of your 9-to-5 to train to be the best at what you do. The thing that should scare you more than anything else is being average. Rise above that fear and do the work it takes to be extraordinary.

Don't think that excellence at your job is limited to just being good at the roles on your job description.

Your talents and skills can help you score at your 9-to-5 too.

I'll give you an example.

I've worked for a Canadian retail giant as an executive assistant for many years. One of the coolest things they implemented in 2017 was "Office Hours" to help bridge the gap between the president and employees. For two hours every quarter, the president opens her door for employees to come in and have a chat or ask a question about the company or their career growth.

When I heard this, I contemplated whether I should even go in. My desk is pretty much right in front of the president's office, but most of the time, I was overlooked or barely acknowledged. I never took offense to it. It is what it is. If you don't show what you bring to the table, you're pretty much invisible. At the time, I had been keeping my head down and trying to nail down my responsibilities, so I understood.

Outside the 9-to-5, I own three companies, one of which is called The WritersBlok (no 'c' on purpose). I had been churning out ghostwritten speeches for celebrities, pro-athletes, and Fortune 500 CEOs. I'm confident enough to say that I'm dope as hell at it. I knew that not a lot of CEOs understand the value of content marketing or working with a speechwriter, so when I see an opportunity, I try to position myself accordingly. When the "Office Hours" came out, I knew that I had an opportunity not just to be seen, but to shine.

I started studying the president. I watched her videos, read her articles, and educated myself on everything there is to know about her. When I walked into her office, I was nervous. But I introduced myself and went for the pitch. After leading with a compliment and referencing her recent New York Times feature, I said, "I know for the past few years, you've delivered countless speeches, led panel discussions, and given amazing presentations."

She nodded her head slowly.

"Well outside the office, I am a professional writer with a genuine interest in working alongside you by ghostwriting some of your key messages. I'd like to take one more thing off your to-do list."

She sat straight up in her chair and smiled. Her response, "Interesting."

I spent the next 10 minutes chatting with her, and our conversation ended with an offer to meet with her PR team. A few days later, I met with the head of public relations. I began working for the president shortly after, up until her term at the company ended. But because I've maintained my relationship with the PR team, naturally, they've asked me to help with content for the president's successor. Hashtag. Winning.

Starting a business isn't the only way to use skills and talents that don't fit into the roles of your job description. Take some time to brainstorm ways you can use the things you're good at to solve a problem or improve a process at your corporate job. When you've come up with some ideas, be bold enough to share them. Speak up, even if your voice shakes, and ask the damn question. The worst that can happen is they say no. And if that's the worst-case scenario, you're already doing better than most people.

If you take nothing else away from this chapter, take this: your corporate success depends entirely on you. No one is going to hand you anything. You have to earn it.

So, act like a boss.

Someone once told me, "No intimidation, no respect." That doesn't mean having a nasty attitude or disrespecting your superiors. It simply means to get a backbone and put your foot down. Be confident. If you act like you're not even supposed to be in the role you have, you'll never get any higher than that. Don't be afraid to open your mouth when you have an idea, question, or concern. I've had meetings with boardrooms full of businessmen who expected me to sit in a corner and eat whatever lines they fed me. But to be honest, that's not my style. As a woman, I know first hand that it's hard to deal with individuals who don't see you as an equal, but over time, I have changed my mentality to channel my inner boss, and now I make sure that I set the tone from the moment I walk into the room. Here are some easy ways to make sure your confidence shines:

- When you feel down, dress up.
- Create a lasting first impression with your introduction, handshake, and smile.
- Be prepared. Do your homework.

- Stand up tall and take up space. Don't ever shrink.
- Fight the urge to fidget, even if it's killing you.
- Look people in the eye when you speak.
- Say what you need to and nothing more. You don't have to fill the silence with chatter.

At every step of your career, from the bottom of the corporate ladder to the peak, always put in the work, go beyond the words in your job description, and bring excellence with you to the office every single day. Don't let that blatant lie that only entrepreneurship takes hustle make you mediocre at your 9-to-5. If the corner office on the top floor is your goal, get to grindin'.

Andrew

Getting anywhere in corporate America, especially if you're young, a minority, and don't have any real network or connections in that world, is a serious grind. I lasted one year in the corporate world. Like, for real, a year. It definitely was not for me. Full transparency—I almost got fired twice because my heart just wasn't in it. There is nothing wrong with corporate America, so don't get me wrong, I just personally had different desires and goals. But the key was I knew I needed to humble myself, continue stacking, and keep learning. In that year I spent working for a major corporation, I saw that succeeding in that world isn't just some walk in the park. The truth is, whether you're clocking in somewhere for 40 hours per week or building a company from the ground up 24/7, it doesn't come easy. If you're finding every step of your journey easy, you're either mad lucky (unlikely) or slacking off. Life should scare you. I talk to so many people who try to overcome fear without realizing fear is a good thing. It means you're pushing yourself to new heights. Who wants to live a perfect, stagnant life? We might as well be robots instead of actual human beings in that case.

Man, listen, if corporate is where you want to be, there's nothing wrong with that. I'm not here for pushing this narrative that everyone should be trying to start a business as if people can't live out their purpose at a 9-to-5. Because you can. I feel like entrepreneurship is the latest trend and everybody's trying to be on it. That just doesn't make sense to me. Entrepreneurship isn't for everybody. You legit have to be a little bit crazy to try and start your own company. It's risky, it costs a ton of time and money, and the reality is that most businesses are going to fall flat on their faces. I'm not a fan of anyone forcing entrepreneurship down someone's throat. Because nine times out of ten, they're probably still broke. Ever notice how many new "internet entrepreneurs and coaches" started popping up recently on social media? Only to find out that they don't own anything. They're salespeople who're taking advantage of people's vulnerabilities. Not everyone, but this is the case for a lot of them. If they'd made any significant money, they would also know how difficult it is and how many stars have to align to build a long-term brand/business. People just aren't practical and don't understand basic math or economics. If everyone were an entrepreneur, there would be no employees in the world.

If everyone had a million dollars, a million dollars would be worthless. This is basic supply and demand, and you see it once you're able to look at things from a different perspective, not just the one that's swallowed by mass-market consumers.

The more I talk to and learn from people, the more I realize I don't want people to look up to something and want more and more. I don't think that's the purpose of our lives. Everyone is so gung-ho on inspiring and for a lot of people, entrepreneurship is up on this pedestal as the way to do that. The internet and all these business coaches and gurus are just pushing that message, and it's making people crazy. They're out here trying to find their "purpose" and the business they're supposed to start when that may not be the life for them.

I don't want to inspire people, man. I'm not trying to make anybody follow my lead into entrepreneurship. I want people to find themselves and decide what success looks like to them. If that's a good job in the corporate world, then dope, do that. Or like, Pauleanna for instance, who runs three brands and still has a 9-to-5. An example that it's okay to be a side-hustler if that's what success looks like to you. She runs a 6-figure business and still finds purpose in a corporate environment. Life could be so amazing working for a company that you care about. In fact, you can be the second, third, fourth, or even twelfth employee and still come out in the top 5% without the stress of the work that comes with being the sole owner and decision maker.

If that's what you want, let's talk about how to get it.

The inside of my head is always full of branding ideas. I mean, when you think about it, everything is branding. Even you. Whether you like it or not, you're always being judged, and you're creating an impression that can either benefit or hurt you. The way you dress and talk, the things you do, the people you hang with, that's all sending a message about you to the world at large. You gotta keep this in mind when you're trying to kill it at your corporate job.

Brand yourself as the dream employee.

On the day I interviewed to work at Pepsi, the interviewer asked me, "Why do you want to work at Pepsi? How do you feel your career here will be?" It's funny because I knew that I needed that job as a stepping stone, but I couldn't just treat it that way. So, I told him what they wanted to hear. At that moment, it was a true statement. I said, "I see myself working here maybe 10, 20, 30 years and just growing through the ranks and continuing to learn." The interviewer was shocked. It was a pretty anti-millennial thing to say. He told me that most people leave within a year or two. Ironically enough, I left after a year. But though I didn't plan to stay in the career my whole life, I knew while I was there, that's how I would work. So, it was an interesting intention, but it was the truth about my work ethic, and that impressed them. I'm almost 90% sure that they said, "Hell yeah, we want him!" And it's because I sounded like the best possible hire.

Before you try and change any system, earn the respect, climb, and then demand change because you'll have leverage. You don't have to listen to me, but I know this works. From your resume to your interview to every single day at your job, you have to make sure that you're showing them that you're the ideal employee. That means you have to understand what the company wants and give it to them. And some of the finer details in that area are going to depend on the job and the company's culture. But some things are true no matter where you go. Every employer wants someone who is passionate about the job and wants to be there. They're looking for someone who's committed and shows up every day on time and ready to go. They're looking for somebody who's eager to learn, over-delivers, and takes initiative. So, if you're trying to create your own destiny and build your own corporate brand, bring your A-game, like you want to take your boss's boss's job. Honestly, if you're that valuable, it's inevitable that you will climb rapidly, and if they get bureaucratic or don't want to play fair, go to their competitor and over-deliver. Trust me, leverage is everything when it comes to branding and growth. When you keep leverage, you win.

Treat the business like it's your own.

Way too many people think of their 9-to-5 as just a j-o-b. Even worse, they go to work and do the minimum required and want the maximum on their checks. They clock in, half-ass their work, scroll Facebook when their manager isn't looking, and clock out at the end of the night. As long as they collect their check, they're good. How unfortunate. Because then they complain that they're not getting paid enough and quit their jobs to start businesses, not understanding they'll just get even less on their own. Don't be that person. You have to treat your job like it's your own business. Act like the little piece of the company you keep running every day is the whole damn business, and if you don't give it your all, the whole thing is going to collapse. If you see your job as just some insignificant piece of the puzzle, that's all you'll ever be.

If you're looking for ways to stand out, look for problems. Yeah, I said it, peel your eyes for the problems that keep coming up. The things your bosses and managers and co-workers are always complaining about.

Turn those problems into solutions.

Fix a problem and watch your brand value grow 10x. This requires you to do more than the minimum requirement. No shit, Sherlock. Yeah, I know it's not in your job description. So what? If you want that job description to get an upgrade and your paycheck to match, you gotta take a little initiative. Bosses hate problems, but they love solutions, and they remember the people who come up with them. It could be something big like pitching your skills to your boss like Pauleanna did with her writing or as simple as finding a way to stop the office copier from making that weird sound that drives everyone crazy. Initiative is always impressive.

And it's the perfect way to make yourself indispensable. That's a major key.

Be so good you're irreplaceable.

An irreplaceable employee has the upper hand when it comes to wage and title negotiations because no company wants to face the struggle of finding a replacement for a top-notch team member. You want to be irreplaceable because your value becomes your leverage. How? Simple. Ask to help with anything you can and take on things outside of your scope. Whatever you take on, be really good at it, even if that means putting in some extra effort to tighten up your skills. Of course, this won't make you completely irreplaceable. I don't know if anything really can. But you can come close, and that's enough to make any employer think twice about letting you go or refusing any requests you might have. With that being said, be prepared for the worst, that way you don't get hit blindly. Always have options available, like other job opportunities. That becomes your leverage when your employer wants to act funny.

Ultimately, all of this can be summed up with this: give a shit about your job and use the hell out of it. That's it. Show up, and work like you care. Every single day. Even if it's a job you took to pay the bills, treat it like it's the dream. Your effort is going to determine your growth. Give nothing, and you'll get nothing. Give your all, and it'll pay off.

JOB – HUNTING 101

Pauleanna

Okay, so you hate your 9-to-5. What are you doing about it? It bothers me when I meet people who complain about their jobs and aren't willing to do anything to change their circumstances. That kind of negativity is so annoying. I know the job market is tough, and holding on to the job you have can seem like the best option. But if your job is draining you, the paycheck is never going to compensate. It's time to get a new one.

That doesn't mean you should just quit and storm out. That's the exact opposite of what you should do. Before you get out of a job you hate, make sure you set yourself up for the smoothest possible transition into one you love. Because the stress of being jobless and broke is no joke. Don't set yourself up to run from one frustration to another. Just like any other career move you'll make, job-hunting takes planning and execution, even if the reason you're looking is that you hate where you are.

In 2014, I was working as an executive assistant to the CEO of a financial institution. The industry wasn't fun for me. I didn't enjoy the job. I was falling asleep to the sound of my heart breaking and waking up feeling less than my best. For eight hours a day, I poured my energy into a job that wasn't fulfilling me. I was doing everything I was supposed to – giving 110%, going above and beyond, and raising my hand for opportunities – but it wasn't enough. I was still miserable. I knew that meant it was time to move on. That job might have been someone else's dream, but there was nothing left in it for me, so I created an exit strategy. I saved nearly $10,000 as a cushion and gave in my resignation.

Side note: saving that $10k wasn't easy. It's hard to adjust to a shoestring budget when you're used to keeping up with the Kardashians. I mean, I was carrying designer purses and rocking brand name everything, so it was a big change. But I became way more conservative with my choices. If I didn't need it, I didn't buy it. The money I would've used to splurge, I dropped it in a savings account instead. It was hard, but I knew what I wanted, and I knew shopping sprees weren't going to help me get it.

I promised myself I would not jump back into the corporate world unless my next opportunity hit specific items on my 'must-have' checklist. It wasn't an easy process. It took forever. I cried, I went broke (even with the $10,000 cushion), and cried some more. I said no to every job offer that fell short because I was determined.

I stuck to my plan, and nine long months later, I had my dream job. I no longer work there, but I built incredibly meaningful and long-lasting relationships, and my old boss is still one of my mentors. The risk was worth it.

If you're unhappy, you hate the people you work with, your ideas aren't being heard, and your workload is increasing while your pay hasn't, you're not tapping into your potential. You deserve to move on. Life is too short to live in complete misery, and 40 years is way too long to be sitting behind a desk doing a job that you hate. But no one is going to take your hand and walk you from the job that's making you miserable into one that makes you feel like a boss. So, I want to give you the tips that helped me through my career transition so you can level up too.

Get clear about what you want.

You know why you hate your current job. Maybe it's the long hours, the low pay, your rude coworkers, or the lack of growth opportunities. For me, it was that the company culture was way too conservative. It wasn't an environment that fostered passion and innovation. Once I got clear on those things, I knew exactly how to focus my job search. Author Danielle Laporte says that you should navigate the decisions in your life based on how you want to feel. Your primary objective should be to feel good. Once you understand what you'll need from a job to feel good about it, you can continue your planning to make it happen, down to the last detail.

So, sit down, and figure out the things that matter to you most. Consider the hours you'd like to work, what kind of opportunities for growth you hope to have, and all the things that will make coming into work every morning worthwhile. Write it all down. When you start your job hunt, make those things a priority. One of the things I discovered in my career transition was the importance of choosing a job based on company culture over salary. Because no amount of money can compensate for a team culture, environment, management style, or company mission that doesn't align with your values. The money will eventually stop being enough. So, as you search for jobs, check out the companies you plan to apply to on Glassdoor and LinkedIn and read reviews from their current and past employees. Allow the things you want to guide your search.

Once you know what you want, get your money right.

I know that when you hate your job, every day feels like torture. Dragging yourself into the office gets harder all the time, and the urge to just walk out keeps getting stronger. But slow down. You can't quit yet because there's nothing cute about being broke.

Trust me, I know. When I say I've been real life broke, it's not even an exaggeration. There were times I wouldn't have been able to catch a bus, much less pay a bill. My bank account was literally empty. I had so much debt and nothing to show for it. And the reality is, I was that broke because I'd made a lot of stupid money decisions. Don't put yourself in that position by quitting your job before you can afford it. As much as I promote running from the job you hate and following your dreams, at the end of the day, you have to be able to pay your rent and keep a roof over your head. Either that, or you can always move back home with mom. Not into that? Okay, then save everything. Even if you have to eat peanut butter and jelly for months. Save an emergency fund so that you can still be financially stable if you decide to tell your boss "peace out." It's what I like to call 'F.U' money, which I learned from former supermodel Tyra Banks. She says, "My mom stayed with my dad for too long because of financial reasons. If she'd just had a little side hustle, a little of her own money, she would have left. So I encourage women to have what I call 'F.U.' money."

There's nothing wrong with wanting it all and then getting it. Personally, I have felt empowered saying (or thinking) F.U. to my boss, my job, my landlord, hey, even my partner. And I could only do that because I put myself in a position to win. Turning your passions into profits is not easy, but your attitude is what will make a huge difference in your ROI.

Building that financial cushion does take sacrifices, and sometimes, a bit of ingenuity. You might have to get creative. Sell some of your gently-used clothing or pick up a part-time hustle for a few extra bucks. Do what it takes. I suggest saving at least six months' rent before jumping ship. Those savings will give you the freedom to search for a new place of employment without panic.

Stay open to all possibilities.

When you know exactly what you want, books will fly off the shelves, certain key players will walk into your life, and opportunities will arise because you're directing your energy towards the life you desire to create. The law of attraction is real. So, keep your eyes, ears, heart, and mind open to the things going on around you. The universe will always present you with signs, but you have to pay close attention. It's important to realize that opportunities are everywhere, though they're not always in the places and through the skillsets you expect. Don't rule anything out.

For example, I'm pretty comfortable with social media, though it's not really a key part of my skillset or career experience. In 2013, the marketing and creative director of a multi-million-dollar company in the food industry contacted me through LinkedIn to ask if I was interested in interviewing for a social media/community manager position. In the end, we both decided it wasn't the right home for me, but the marketing director left the door wide open and said if I were ever looking for work in that field he would help me in any way he could through his contacts. I took that as a sign that something I do for fun could turn into a whole new career path. This could be true for you too. Make a list of what you're good at. It could pay the bills if you learn to master your talent.

Switch to an industry where you can fill a gap.

Staying open means keeping your eyes peeled for opportunities. When I left my banking job, I knew I wanted to switch industries. I went from the banking industry to high-end fashion retail. It felt like a good fit for me as a place where I could bring my creative skills to the table on the executive side. It was a good move for me. At one point, I also considered jumping into the tech world, a male-dominated space that needs more female professionals. If you're looking for a career change, definitely consider moving to a new industry so you can add value and bring a wealth of knowledge to the profession.

Go for it, even if you're not built for it.

Part of staying open to possibilities is being bold enough to apply to jobs you're not qualified for. Does that sound crazy? It isn't. Way too often, we rule ourselves out of opportunities because we can't check off every item on the job description's skills list. Many of us have been programmed to believe that we don't have the power to choose what we want in our lives, but the reality is that we do! I dropped out of college my second year, so technically I wasn't "qualified" to do a lot of things I currently do now. I built my experience in other ways like building a personal brand and blog which opened so many doors.

I didn't go to school for professional writing. It's all self-taught. I developed from an amateur blogger (age 21) to a nationally-published journalist (age 22) to a best-selling author (age 26) to a celebrity/CEO ghostwriter (now) which has become a significant portion of my side income. Same with public speaking. No one "taught" me how to become a public speaker. I learned to start before I was ready. Listen, start somewhere. Take a step anywhere but backward. If there's a job you're interested in, but you're not totally skilled for, be prepared to do the work to prove why they should hire you. Take an online or entry-level course to develop the skills you don't have. Practice those skills often. If you're not good at something, do the work to get good at it.

Repackage your resume.

The rule still applies, "Your reputation is worth more than any resume." But it still doesn't hurt to put one together. Not just any resume, though. It needs to be killer. If you're getting ready to find a new job, it's time to get your resume right. How "right" is defined depends on the industry you're applying to. The kind of resume you can put together in creative industries might be different from what you present when you apply for a job in healthcare or finance. Do some research and figure out what will impress in your industry and consider what will appeal to the companies you're applying to.

I once had an interview with a cool company in digital media. At the end of my meeting, I presented a saddle-stitched book, created by me, which included six ways I could improve the founder's productivity. Listen, I don't play. The job market is competitive, so you better come correct.

You need to stand out. You may not be able to present a portfolio style resume at every interview, but you should be finding ways to package yourself so that you stand out. Let the world know how dope you are by updating your LinkedIn profile, utilizing social media, creating a cool video resume, or signing up for CareerBuilder or Monster with a profile that's all the way together.

Stay focused.

Following any of those steps will matter if you don't stay focused. Job-hunting can be a long process. You could find a job just weeks after you quit, or like my story, it could take months. Through it all, keep your focus. It all goes back to your core desired feelings. You aren't just chasing your goal of a good job; you are chasing the feeling you'll receive once you get it. Remember, the primary objective is always to feel good. You'll face roadblocks, have interviews that suck, have seemingly great opportunities fall through. Just keep putting one foot in front of the other and keep your eyes on the prize.

Now, prep time is pointless if you're not ready when it's game time. You've decided what you want, saved a financial cushion, created a killer resume, and kept your eyes peeled for opportunities, but none of that matters if you bomb in every interview. Nailing the interview is what ultimately gets you the job. I don't just mean impressing the interviewer with your answers and skills, though that's really important too. But it's important to realize that the interview is an exchange—your chance to learn whether the job is what you want and need.

You're interviewing them too.

Valerie Jarrett, lawyer and ex-White House Senior Advisor to former US President Obama put it perfectly: "When you're in a job interview, you should remember it's a two-way street. Yes, you're trying to make the best case for why you should be hired, but they need to make a case for why this is an environment where you're gonna do well." She's right. Once you've answered all the interviewer's questions and they get to the part where they ask if you have any questions, say yes. You should have questions.

Go back to that 'must-have' list you created, and make sure you know whether the job offers you all of that. Sitting in the room with the interviewer, you're going to get answers to questions no website 'About' page can give you.

And when they ask you why you're the right candidate, speak up.

Seriously, the interview is not the time to be fake-humble. Yes, keep it polite, but don't be shy. Interviewers are asking why they should hire you because they actually want to know. So, you better tell them. I once interviewed for a fantastic media job, and their final request was to brag about myself. I found it kind of odd, and it caught me completely off guard, but I did exactly what I was told and bragged about my accomplishments until I was blue in the face. And you know what? That same day, I received a phone call for a second interview, and they told me it was my killer pitch that got me the golden position. Remember, if you can speak about yourself and your work confidently, you can shine more brightly than you ever will on a resume. So, get comfortable speaking about yourself and never undersell. When you get a chance to brag, do it. Because it just might be the thing that gets you the job.

If you're right for the job, make sure you get paid.

So, negotiate your salary. Just because an offer was put out doesn't mean you have to take it. Before you go into the interview, you should know the average salary for a person in that position with your level of experience. Make sure you do your homework so that you don't end up underpaid. This is especially important for women. I read in a Forbes article that when Linda Babcock was doing the research for her book Women Don't Ask, she found out that only 7% of women negotiated salaries when they first enter the workplace, compared to 57% of men. Ladies, don't leave money on the table that should be in your bank account. Evaluate what you bring to the table, and if you truly believe you deserve more than what they're offering you, it's in your best interest to express that opinion.

Bozoma Saint John, Uber's CBO, gets right to the point with her advice on salary negotiations. She told Glamour in an interview, "Give the [salary] number first and make it high as hell. You know what the range is. How can they lowball you after they know what your number is?" Closed mouths don't get fed. If you just settle for what's handed to you, that's all you'll ever get.

If you're still struggling with the idea of negotiating your salary and your worth to your employer, add these two books to your reading list: Nice Girls Don't Get Rich and Nice Girls Don't Get the Corner Office. Those titles never lied. You can't be too "nice" to ask for what you want and deserve. Those books will help you learn how to speak up and get your coins.

The ultimate goal with job-hunting isn't to get a job, it's to get the job that's right for you. Yes, sometimes you take a job because you've got to pay the bills, cover the rent, and keep the lights on. But at some point, your career has to stop being about survival and start being about finding the space you thrive in. What you'll need to make that happen, more than anything else, is confidence. Don't let fear or frustration guide your job search.

Chapter 8:
A Brand Within a Brand

BEYOND LINKEDIN

Pauleanna

I love LinkedIn. I think it's a dope and super underrated platform. One of the things I encourage my mentees to do early on is to set up a LinkedIn profile. And not some sloppy, rushed bio. You gotta take your time and make that profile bomb as hell because a good profile is like a resume you never have to send out. There are recruiters all over LinkedIn searching for top talent, and if your profile is on point, they just might slide into your inbox with the job opportunity of your dreams. It's happened to me a time or two because I've invested time and energy developing a profile that really lets me shine. I have a solid bio and job history, tons of endorsements on my key skills, over 100 recommendations from past employers and clients, and a network that's more than 500 strong. My LinkedIn game is no joke. Yours shouldn't be either.

Get your LinkedIn poppin'.

If you're not signed up yet, get on it. Once you've got your profile up and running, make sure your summary highlights your accomplishments and the value you bring. The bio should be about you, yes, but more specifically, about how you can be of use to potential employers. Let your personality shine, speak the language of your industry, and always keep it professional. Don't skimp on the descriptions of your past jobs either. Just like on a resume, take the time to paint a picture of the ways you were amazing at your job. Go on and brag a little. Let people know what you're working with. And once you've done your part, seek out endorsements and recommendations from others. Sometimes, all it takes to get a glowing review from a manager or colleague is to ask. Those recommendations could be the co-sign that pushes a potential employer to hire you. But LinkedIn is even more than a job board. It's an amazing tool for networking too.

Use social media right, and your online presence can turn the key on mentorship.

I recently spoke to Meg Garlinghouse, LinkedIn's head of Social Impact for a Forbes article. We talked about how LinkedIn users could turn their connections into mentorship opportunities, a key resource for young professionals. LinkedIn is currently piloting a feature called Career Advice that would connect members looking for advice with appropriate business and industry leaders to answer their questions. That feature won't launch for a while, but you can still use LinkedIn to connect with professionals in your field and begin building relationships that could one day lead to mentorships.

But LinkedIn isn't the end all and be all of professional social networking. There are so many dope platforms built to help young people in the early stages of their career find mentors. Sites like meetup.com and tenthousandcoffees.com make the process easy. Through these platforms, you can meet experts In your industry who will sit down with you—or chat with you on the phone or over Skype—and give you advice and answer your questions. But remember, give as much as you take. When you use these platforms, bear in mind the things you can offer and the ways you can be useful to your connections and potential matters.

Of course, not everyone you meet has to be a mentor. Linkedin, Meetup, and Ten Thousand Coffees, along with all your regular social media platforms, are great for making friends, meeting like-minded people, and connecting with potential collaborators.

Start sowing the seeds of friendship.

Use your social presence to start what's called "friend farming" — which is turning strangers into friends. Real friends. You want to connect with people who vibe on the same frequency. If you're using your social media effectively and projecting what you want to attract, these friends will be easy to find. Building those connections and being a genuine, supportive friend to the people you meet online will help you develop an invaluable network and build some serious social capital. Social capital can help you fill in gaps that would be otherwise hard to fill.

Let me explain. When I started my businesses, I didn't have anything. No financial backing, no business degree. There were times I wasn't even 100% sure what I was doing. But I understood the importance making meaningful connections, and because of my network, I've been able to live the life of my dreams, including writing my book, speaking on national stages, working with celebrity clients, and becoming a contributor to Forbes.com.

Don't count out the big three.

I'm talking about Facebook, Twitter, and Instagram. I don't think some people truly understand the power of the digital market and how it gives you the ability to jump into conversations and make friends around the world. I'm so amazing at networking on these platforms it's not even fair. The way I navigate and connect is beyond average. I don't get on my phone just to scroll. Every time I open those apps, it's with a strategy and a plan. A lot of the press I've gotten has come from just being connected to the right people. When people ask me how I get featured, I simply reply, "Easy. Pay attention." Most reporters, writers, talk show producers, and editors seek talent online. Follow the right people. Be all up in their digital space. I got my Global News (a national Canadian broadcast station) feature because I replied to a tweet from one of their reporters, and we scheduled a call and chatted that same day. Whether you're looking for press, collaborators, mentorship, or job opportunities, make sure you follow the big names in your industry and connect with other people who do what you do.

Alright, so you're following good people and you're making connections. Cool. Now what? Work it to your advantage.

Take advantage of how much "insider info" social media gives you.

Whether you meet someone online or off, get to creeping. Don't play like you don't creep. We all do it. I'm just telling you to do it with a purpose now. Learn things about your new connection like their birthday, new jobs announcements, family events, business ideas. Paying attention and being able to reference these details when you communicate with them is vital to nurturing the relationship. Be intentional about communication too. A simple strategy I use is a contact plan. I have a tack board with a map in my bedroom, and at the beginning of every month, I pin the names of people I need to catch up with on that board so that it's visible daily. I schedule time in my calendar to catch up with friends — online and off, new and old — even if it's just a ten-minute touch base via Skype.

Social media is also a very helpful tool to use before offline networking. If you're going to a conference or a networking event and you have access to the guest list via social media, make sure you take some time to study who's going to be in attendance. This way, you can find out who the key players are (to you) and do some research on them. For instance, let's say I ran into Gabrielle Union at a social event. Naturally, I'm going to lead with a mention of her new book or her activism for women's issues. She'd be much more interested in what I have to offer if I can show that I know what's important to her.

But don't get so caught up in using social media to connect with others that you forget to carefully curate your online presence and develop your personal brand online.

Brand yourself.

No, personal brands aren't just for entrepreneurs. Corporate professionals should be building their brand online too. By brand, I mean the way you represent yourself, your skills, and your accomplishments. Yes, keep it professional, but let your personality and expertise shine. Ultimately, be yourself.

I recently had Toronto City Hall reach out and ask me to come through and teach a group of young women who aspire to become politicians how to brand themselves on social media. I'm no expert by any means, but I often get requests like these because of my transparency (online). It is possible to get opportunities for just being yourself. The problem is, too many people are trying to be someone else. Ditch that. There's a reason it's called personal branding.

But there are a few kinds of posts I've found are universally useful for this kind of thing:

1. Share cool resources.

Whatever your field of expertise is, share helpful resources, news, or events in the industry that would interest other people in your field. You'll look like you're in the know, and you'll also mark yourself as valuable.

2. Share projects you're working on.

If you're not bound by any confidentiality agreements or won't compromise your employer in any way, share with your audience the dope projects you're working on or exciting accomplishments you're pulling off at work.

3. Take your audience to work with you.

Take it a step further and take your audience into the office. Again, make sure it's cool with your boss and the company policies, but shoot a little Instagram video of your office space, a work conference, or a team outing.

4. Show love to other professionals.

Is someone you know doing something awesome? Shout them out and highlight their accomplishments. Part of your brand should be giving the spotlight to people in your network.

5. Cross-promote on your social media channels.

The content that shines on Instagram (pictures and video) is different from the things that work well on Twitter (short quotes), and Facebook (conversational posts and storytelling). Cross-promote your various social media channels to encourage people to connect with you on all your platforms so they can get a full picture of you and your brand.

Remember that your social media represents you in front of millions of people. That means potential employers, recruiters, collaborators, press outlets, and colleagues. People see it before they even meet you in person. So, don't ever get it twisted — social media absolutely matters. The sooner you master it, the better.

Chapter 9:
The Struggle Continues

⸺⸻⸺

A DISMAL OUTLOOK

⸺⸻⸺

Pauleanna

Your 9-to-5 doesn't suck. Your attitude does. I've told you enough stories about my struggles with corporate jobs that were less than ideal for you to know that I've been through it. But the reality remains, if you look at your job as something that sucks, that's how it's always going to feel. If you're an entrepreneur trying to turn your side hustle into a main hustle, or you're committed to corporate and trying to get to the top, the job you're in right now is an important part of your journey. So, you better get that attitude in check.

Get your head in the game from the minute you wake up.

The more you speak negativity into your life, the higher you build a wall between you and your destiny. If the first thing you think when you wake up in the morning is, "I hate this job," guess what kind of day you're going to have. Words and thoughts have enormous power, and if you don't start filtering your language and talking to yourself with more positivity and respect, you'll keep walking in circles. So, my first suggestion is to start each day with 5-10 minutes of silence. At the very least, give God thanks for breathing air into your lungs. Be grateful for the fact that you have a damn job to wake up to when other people are still searching endlessly. Take a second to breathe and refrain from starting your day caught up in the false impressions of someone's Instagram or Facebook profile. Get some gratitude and perspective before you leave your bed so that when your feet hit the ground, you can move with purpose and intention.

Once you get into the office, give your best effort. Not just some days, but every damn day. Yes, when you're tired. Yes, when your manager is a jerk. Yes, when the work is boring you half to death.

Don't ask for more when you haven't even mastered less.

The "more" that you want is going to come with days when you're tired, when you have to deal with jerks, and when you're not excited about everything on your to-do list. If you can't push through now, what's going to happen when the stakes are higher? Pushing through now is like flexing the muscles that will help you persevere when struggles come at your dream job or in your own business. Consider this practice for the big win. At every stage and every age, you need to be productive. Master this season so you can take the lesson and move on.

My dad always says, "Baby, do what you have to do so you can do whatever the hell you want to do." He's right. While grinding away at jobs that I wasn't entirely thrilled about, I pushed through with my chin up and walked out at 5:00 pm knowing that I could work on my passions from 6:30 pm to midnight. I knew a corporate job would give me the ability to fund my dream and grow my business.

Remember the story I told you about Courtney Sanders, my friend who used the boring tasks at her 9-to-5 to spend time listening to business podcasts and audiobooks? Well, she got way more out of her corporate gig than study time. While she was grinding away for 40 hours or more every week, she was stacking her savings and investing in her business. Courtney always knew she wanted to be an entrepreneur, but she had to start somewhere. Within a year of starting her business Think and Grow Chick, her earnings surpassed her corporate salary. A huge part of that success came from the leverage having a 9-to-5 in the same industry as her business offered her. The job made the dream possible.

I was in the same boat. But what I got from a lot of my jobs was the money to let me do what I love. When I was writing my first book, I wasn't making any money off it. Books don't earn you a dime until they're published. I couldn't eat off my book until I finished it, and I couldn't write the book if I wasn't paying my bills. So I went to work and grinded through my day job so I could afford to spend every spare minute I had writing a book. It took me four years. That's four years I spent in jobs that weren't ideal so that I could fulfill my lifelong goal of writing a novel. And in 2014, I released it worldwide.

Learn to see how your 9-to-5 feeds your dream.

For you, it may be leverage or experience like Courtney, industry contacts like Andrew, or straight up cash like me. Whatever it is, you have to start seeing how your 9-to-5 helps you get closer to where you want to be. Drop the idea that it's an obstacle and look at it as a stepping stone. It's just a stop on your journey, so milk it for what it's worth until you can move on.

But don't coast. Make excellence your reputation wherever you're at.

How you show up and the level of commitment you bring to everything you do matters — and that includes the job you don't love. People are always watching. Bosses, colleagues, clients. They're paying attention to you. So, if you're rolling into work every day with a nasty attitude and half-assing your work, you're marking yourself as someone that can't be relied on, and a reputation like that is hard to shake. Always make sure you are the best at what you do and show others what you've got. I know you have it in you, so don't make a lasting bad impression. You don't know who has their eye on you and what power they have to get you closer to your goals.

I know that the perspective shift isn't always enough though. Some days, you come into the office, and you feel like one more minute with that job, those coworkers, and that irritating manager is going to make you quit on the spot. I've had those days, and I have a few tips I picked up over the years that helped me keep my sanity and my job.

Make your space feel like a sanctuary.

Whether you're in a big office or a tiny cubicle, it's a good idea to personalize your space by surrounding yourself with things that make you smile. It can be as simple as a vase of flowers, photos of your family and friends, or posters of inspirational sayings. Not only will those things put a smile on your face when you really need one, but they'll give you a chance to control at least a little piece of your day.

Get rid of the mess.

Flowers and photos are personal, garbage and piles of papers are not. There's nothing more frustrating than working in a messy environment. If your office doesn't have a "clean desk" policy, implement one for yourself. Save your coffee money and invest in a few organizational tools that will help you find things more easily and work more efficiently. It's possible that some of the irritation you're feeling at work could simply because there's just way too much stuff around you.

Take a mental vacation.

No matter how crappy your job feels, remember it's mind over matter. So, go ahead and check out of the office for a bit, just in your head. Close your eyes and take a few minutes to escape for a little bit. Whether you imagine your happy place, repeat mantras or affirmations out loud, meditate, or just simply count, allow your mind to get away for a short while so you can get back to work.

Hold on to your truths.

Your success will only be as big as your appetite, so revisit your vision, the purpose we talked about. Sit and reflect for a few minutes about how this job is going to help you fulfill that. Keep your mind on that. Think back to your vision board and shift your focus onto your career goals. Think about how amazing you will feel once you achieve the next positive step in the right direction.

A HIGHER CALLING

Andrew

Your job is fine. Your ungrateful attitude and unwillingness to play the long game is what's making you miserable. Years ago, when I was working in corporate America, I could say that my job sucked, but that would be a lie. I worked with Pepsi, a Fortune 500 company. I can't sit here and pretend that wasn't an amazing opportunity. And somebody built for the corporate world would probably have been excited to go into that office every day and sit in the seat I was taking up and do that work. That wasn't me. I legit wanted to quit that job at a point, but it wasn't really because of the job. It was because I wanted to be somewhere else. I wanted something different. I wasn't made to be in corporate. The "problem" was me. Once I stopped focusing on how much the job wasn't what I wanted, and started seeing how there were things I wanted and needed at that job, man, the whole game changed.

I can hear you saying, "But Drew, my job isn't Pepsi. There's nothing I want here. This job ain't shit." I don't want to hear it. Cause I'm willing to bet if I sat down and talked to you for five minutes, I could tell you ten ways you could get something valuable out of that job you think is useless. You better humble out. Only arrogance would let you believe that you don't have anything to learn from an established company. And if you don't get humble and see that, life is going to cut you down to size real quick.

We've got pages of advice and tips in this book to help you figure out how to get something valuable out of every job you work on the way to the one you want. If you put this book down and still believe that there's nothing for you in your job, that's a choice you're making. I want to challenge you to make a different choice right now. Start by recognizing that almost every successful person you've ever admired has been right where you are, in a job that they didn't care for. The difference between what you're doing and what they did? They realized that every moment and experience is part of the journey to where they want to be, and you don't get to skip ahead.

If my story and Pauleanna's aren't enough proof, let me give you some more examples:

I got a chance to sit down and talk to Tola Lawal. She's the founder of Gyrl Wonder, a non-profit organization out in New York City that helps young girls reach their goals. And Tola's killing the game. Gyrl Wonder was voted the #1 organization for girls of color in 2017. But she didn't just wake up in that position one day. Like Pauleanna, she still has a 9-5. She's the Assistant Director of College Success at a charter high school. I asked her why, and she said that as an entrepreneur, she really benefited from having a day job to balance out her entrepreneurial ventures. She explained it like this:

"I actually consider my job my side job. I consider my not-for-profit my full-time job. My job is my side hustle. It allows me to invest in my passions. From nonprofit and my brands, the goal is just to build myself as a leader in whatever space I am in right now. That is my full-time job. My 9-to-5 just funds that — my dreams."

The dream is big. I mean it's pretty damn impressive. Over the last two years, Tola's brought in Bree from America's Next Top Model to teach yoga classes, took her mentees to Black Girls Rock, and in the second year of programming, her mentees got full rides to colleges. I mean, she's really putting in work. But she's dreaming even bigger, and her day job is helping her learn the things she's gonna need to make it happen.

Cash all the checks you can from your job, and not just the ones that have a dollar sign on them.

"I eventually do want to take my experience with the youth and create a youth consumer department at a big brand. I'm not too far removed from marketing and entertainment. I would love to create a youth consumer department or go to youth culture at Instagram or something like that. I'm using this opportunity to get hands-on experience and information from our students, so I can take it and create some dope shit with a bigger brand."

Tola gets it. She knows that her job gives her leverage, whether it's the cash to fund her business or experience to help her level up. If she can make a day job work for her, then so can you.

Here's another example. Shawn Johnson, a programming entrepreneur that I met when I moved out to ATL, got a pretty late start in the game at 17. Sounds crazy, but he explained that 17 is a lot older than most people in the business start getting to know computers. But he knew he had to learn the ropes, so he asked his Dad for a computer. Here's how that went:

"When [my Dad] saw how much a computer costs, he was like 'Yeah, no.' So, we had to work that out later. I actually got a credit card at 17 and bought an Amiga 500, which was my first computer. It was something that I thought about and then made it happen. But at that point, technology seemed unapproachable. So, I ended up taking a couple of jobs where we worked with computers, not like a programmer, but I was around it enough."

And Shawn didn't stop there. After studying programming at Devry, he talked his way into a job at an IT Help Desk.

"I was doing help desk support. I wouldn't shut up. Like, 'Hey, I program. Hey, I program.' Finally one of the VPs was like, 'I get it you want to program.' And he gave me an opportunity. He let me do a programming test, and I failed it so hard, like really, really hard. But I didn't let that set me back. I acknowledged that it happened, but I decided I was going to take the opportunity and do whatever I could with it. They gave me a programming job, and then a month later, someone else gave me a programming job, and I just worked my way up the ladder, doing more advanced technology."

From there, he went from programmer to in-house consultant to entrepreneur. He's now the founder of Mobile App Hero and he teaches hundreds of students app development every year. But it was a process. He didn't just wake up with his dream job. He had the magic formula.

Humility + hustle + Knowing when to speak the hell up = A pathway to success.

Shawn literally started from the bottom, hustled in every role, learned everything he could, and then worked his way to the top. But imagine if Shawn had felt like those basic computer jobs or that IT Help Desk position weren't close enough to programming for him, that they sucked too much. Shawn is proof of what humility and strategic planning will get you.

Shawn has now got his eye on another industry, and he's taking the same approach to get where he wants to be. He explains it like this: "So many people want to be the boss that they are not good workers. There are certain things you have to learn, and you can only learn through experience. It's cool to want to build this big thing and be the boss or disrupt an industry, but you need relevant boots-on-the-ground experience in the industry. I'm working on a project in fashion, I'm running two startups. I'm ready to go and intern for somebody else because nothing that I have makes me qualified in those other industries."

So if you're still sitting there whining about your job instead of making a list of ways to turn it into something that works for you the way Pauleanna, Tola, Shawn, me and a bunch of other smart entrepreneurs have, I don't know what else to tell you other than to get it together. How? Hint: read the next chapter.

Chapter 10:
Work that 9-5 to the Max

⚜

ON-THE-JOB EDUCATION

⚜

Pauleanna

There's more to your 9-5 than the paycheck, even if that job isn't what you want to do with the rest of your life. If you hope to one day create something of your own—whether it may be to launch an idea, create an event, or develop a business or a brand, I can't think of a better opportunity to get ready than to take in all the gems from your job. If you want to build a successful business, you need to see how one is run.

Remember, I didn't go to school for business. Everything I know about running a business, I learned outside of the classroom. A huge part of that education came from keeping my eyes wide open at my job. As a receptionist and executive assistant, my role meant administrative tasks. Filing papers, taking calls, managing calendars. Nothing that would really bring me closer to knowing everything I needed to know to run multiple businesses. But I kept my eyes and ears open for the things happening beyond my desk. I watched and studied how the Finance and Marketing departments run. The things I learned from just paying attention have helped me make sure my businesses stayed in the black, and my marketing and PR have been on point. I took what they did, adapted it to my needs and made it work for my brands. Every single day was preparing me for launching a business of my own.

Treat your 9-to-5 like research and data.

The next time you're tempted to complain about your job, try changing your perspective. If you're an aspiring entrepreneur, going to work is like going to business school for free. Imagine that every single day you can study how a major company runs. You get to see concepts in practice, what business strategies work, and which ones flop. And you get paid for it. That's a win-win situation. So, show up every day prepared to pay attention.

Sit in on meetings, even the ones you weren't invited to.

Within limits, obviously. There are meetings that you can't slide into unnoticed. But go to the ones you're supposed to, and the ones that you can slip into. Some are going to be boring, but you might be surprised at the gems that get dropped in those meetings. So, pay attention to the things your superiors and colleagues are saying and take notes.

Request some meetings of your own with the office bigwigs.

I used to schedule informational interviews with executives on all levels and analyzed every department. You might be surprised at who says yes to meeting with you if you just ask. Even 10 minutes picking a departmental manager or executive's brain can be beneficial. If you don't ask, the answer is guaranteed to be no. Just make the request.

Just listen.

It seems like such simple advice, but it's seriously underrated. You don't always have to ask questions to learn things. You hear better with your mouth shut. When you're around your manager, pay attention to how they talk and what they say. Listen to how your colleagues talk about and react to your boss. Just from those simple interactions, you'll learn how a boss effectively communicates with and inspires their staff—or doesn't.

President of Lord & Taylor, Liz Rodbell, is big on this advice. She said, "Your bosses and colleagues will have a lot to teach you—even the ones you don't particularly like. Be open to interaction and conversation with them. Watch their actions and their processes. Whether you're learning from them what to do or what behaviors to avoid like the plague."

When you get a chance to rub shoulders with bosses, rub 'em.

As an executive assistant, I've had the chance to be around a few industry leaders. One day, I'm in the same room as Joe Mimran, the Canadian fashion designer and entrepreneur behind Club Monaco and Joe Fresh. He is also one of the dragons on Canadian business reality show Dragons' Den (similar to Shark Tank). The next, I'm sharing space with Bill Gates and Justin Trudeau. But whether it's the leader of a country, a CEO, or the president of the company you work for, take advantage of the opportunities to be in the presence of people who are levels above you.

Every day when you roll into the office, approach it as a learning opportunity. Pay attention to the details, look for the openings, and most importantly, stop complaining. Every time you do, you show that you're not a winning player and you're not ready to operate at the next level. Before you can make any kind of leap, you need to make sure you're getting everything you can from right where you're at. Trust me, the single most important factor that contributed to my success is the ability to humble myself, get mentored by my bosses and find the lessons in every day.

Andrew

For budding entrepreneurs, a day job is like free business school. And though I had graduated with an MBA, there are just some things you can't learn in a lecture hall. A lot of business practices and theories, especially things like sales, are one thing on paper, but it's not the same as actually doing it. I knew if I wanted to kill it with the O Agency and make it a profitable business, sales was one of the things I was going to need to master. If I couldn't sell potential clients on the business, nothing else I did would matter, right?

So, Pauleanna's advice about using your day job for research and data— so real. In my year at Pepsi, I dived into my sales role. Every time I attempted a sale, whether I nailed it or failed, I was taking notes. What worked? What didn't? What made clients excited and what turned them off? What kinds of clients went for certain techniques? You better believe I was building my own database of sales knowledge.

You don't have to reinvent the wheel.

Sales is an invaluable skill, no matter what kind of business you're starting. And even if you plan to stay in the corporate world, at the very least, you'll know how to market yourself. If you've got a chance to learn sales from your current job, take it. Even if it's not the department you're working in, do what Pauleanna did, and watch what the sales reps and execs do and say. And don't just count on what you can learn on your own. Most companies have sales manuals and processes that they've been using for years, decades even, because they work. Pepsi did. They've been around for over 100 years. I think by now they've got their sales strategy pretty well hammered out, and they've got the budget to invest in working out any issues that come up. Why would anyone pass up a chance to learn from that?

Whether you're in sales, marketing, front-line customer service, accounting, or management, you've got an amazing chance to learn from a business that has systems that work. Learn them. Get good at the ones you get paid for, and then get a little nosy and learn the other skills that keep the office running. When you create a business of your own, you may have to bend and adjust those processes a bit to fit your needs, but at least the foundation is laid. Don't waste time starting from scratch when you have an opportunity to build on something that already works. I mean, I'm using some of the sales processes that I learned at Pepsi with the O Agency to this day.

While I was paying attention to the practices that kept Pepsi running, I was also people watching. You can't run a business unless you get people. No amount of Googling and research is going to help you understand people the way that being around them does.

Become a people watcher.

It's all about perspective, right. The more time you spend around people, the more you learn about them, and the more you can understand how they think and what they want. Whenever this subject comes up, I always think of Tony Robbins. That man is so successful, and I think that has a lot do with the fact that he's spent decades in different countries around different cultures and people. So, he has the perspective to see and understand people in a way that a lot of others can't.

That was something I wanted to nail down, and working at Pepsi really helped me do that. I spent the first ten years of my life mostly immersed in Vietnamese culture. My parents and their culture were my biggest influence. Then when we moved to a predominantly Black area, that became the culture I spent the most time around. I got to know what was dope in those circles and what would offend people. Right there, another demographic I got to learn about. When I started at Pepsi, I got a chance to learn about a different group of people—corporate white America. Because I knew I wanted to build my business and be really successful, I knew I'd have to be able to speak the language and understand the thinking of that group. We're pushing hard for diversity in business, and I think that's dope, but the reality is, right now, that investors, venture capitalists, other business owners, potential clients fall into that category.

So, being able to people watch at Pepsi was definitely an asset for me. I got to see first-hand some of what corporate white Americans really thought and believed and saw how they operated. I realized that not all of the stereotypes and expectations I had were legit. And if I had gone into business thinking I knew what was up with a whole group of people just based on my expectations, I would have been dead wrong.

Pay attention to people. Your bosses, your coworkers, the clients you speak to. Learn what matters to them. What drives them? What makes them act and think the way they do? Have legit conversations. For real, just talk to people. Entrepreneurship can be lonely, and sometimes, it can feel like every conversation you have is going to make or break your business. But at a day job, it's a chance to just interact with people for the sake of getting to understand them.

The funny thing is, the more people you talk to, the more relationships you build. And those relationships can end up being key to your success in the future.

Make connections that count.

Going into a corporate office is like attending a networking event every day. You've got a chance to connect with people in different areas of the business. If you build genuine relationships, you may be able to leverage them down the road. I'll give you an example. While I was working at Pepsi, I communicated directly with the companies and managers in the sale zone they assigned me to. While I was calling them to make sales, I got to know them and learned a little about their needs. And though they didn't know it, I was brainstorming in my head ways that the O Agency could be useful to them. It paid off. One of the first clients I had after I left Pepsi was a 7/11 that I did a branding project for. Because I'd built a relationship with the manager there, I was ready to make my pitch, and they were down to work with me.

Your 9-to-5 is a step on your journey, no matter what your goal destination is. I think as millennials, we're too caught up in the end goal, and we want to rush through the early parts, but that doesn't make sense. That corporate experience is important, even if you want to be an entrepreneur someday. Myleik Teele tweeted something the other day that sums this up: "A lot of young entrepreneurs that I see struggling are doing so because they didn't take the time to work for someone else first. Let someone teach you the ropes. It's FREE learning from their mistakes." She's right. Learn and grow where you are so when it's time for you to do your own thing, you'll be ready.

DOLLARS AND SENSE

Pauleanna

I may be doing well financially now, but in my early 20s, my finances were a hot mess. I'll never forget the day I checked my account balance, and the statement said $2.09. Nobody would have known because I was carrying $2,000 purses, but I didn't even have $5 to my name. Meanwhile, I had a mountain of bills, creditors constantly calling me, and nothing to pay them with. I just wanted to cry because I felt so defeated. I was anxious about my future. Not just my career, but financially. I was living life in the red.

A famous rapper once said, "Mo money, mo problems." But if you've ever had no money, you know just how many problems that comes with. And while you're dealing with the bills, the debt, and not being able to afford the life you dream of, you're busy trying to keep up appearances to match society's image of success.

You gotta quit trying to keep up with the Kardashians.

I get it. We all want the nice things we're being sold a million different ways every day. But you're not a Kardashian, and you're just going to put yourself in a hole if you keep trying to live like one. I was so depressed when I was broke because I was constantly trying to fit in, and the pressure of that was unreal. Do not watch social media and get caught up thinking "I want that too" because the person you're admiring probably doesn't have it in real life. Luxury car rentals, knock-off Birkins, and gold-plated chains aren't that hard to come by. Don't get caught up. Your lane is yours and yours alone. It's time to focus on you.

Get your money mindset right, ASAP.

Our generation needs to step up the financial literacy and shift the way we think about finances. According to Forbes, 43% of millennials are still financially dependent on their parents. Damn, we need to do better, y'all. And not just when it comes to earnings (though it doesn't hurt to earn more). But your attitude towards money, and the way you manage it is what really changes the game.

I've got a small library of books on personal finance that have helped me get my money mindset right. If you're ready to start digging your way out of debt, hit up Amazon and pick up a few of these dope reads:

Money: A Love Story – Kate Northrup

This book will help you figure out where your mind is at on the subject of money, examine your current financial situation, and figure out a plan to get to your money goals.

Get Rich Lucky Bitch – Denise Duffield-Thomas

This no-nonsense author helps you figure out the mental blocks that are keeping your wallet and pockets empty so you can stop thinking from a place of lack and start pulling in the money you deserve.

The Law of Divine Compensation – Marianne Williamson

If you're a person who believes in spirituality or lives by faith, this book is an amazing reminder of God's promise of abundance and prosperity and gives advice on how to overcome financial stress.

It's Your Money: Becoming a Woman of Independent Means – Gail Vaz-Oxlade

Famed financial expert Gail Vaz-Oxlade serves up advice on recognizing your financial power and how to deal when money troubles arise. You can count on her usual straight-up delivery to help you get your butt in gear.

The Money Book for the Young, Fabulous & Broke – Suze Orman

Suze Orman talks right to us millennials about the financial issues that matter to us most: credit card debt, credit scores, student loans, buying a house, figuring out insurance, and getting your money right if you're self-employed.

Nice Girls Don't Get Rich – Lois P. Frankel

In this book, Frankel offers proven financial coaching tips and helps people (women in particular) spot the 75 mistakes that are keeping them broke.

A few dollars go a long way.

While I was reading up and taking notes from those books back in my early 20s, I made a decision to start saving. At the time, I was barely bringing in any money with my little entry-level job, but I started where I could. Twenty dollars every month. It wasn't much, but to me it was everything. I knew my meager savings wasn't going to buy me a house like I wanted, but it was a start.

When I could raise the bar, I did, eventually saving $50 per month, then $100. Now that I'm making a good amount of money, I'm able to save as much as $500 every month. The point is, start saving what you can, even if it's small. Over time, if you're making other smart decisions about money, that amount will grow and push you closer to your goals all the time.

Capitalize on those company perks.

That bi-weekly check is going to help you fatten up your savings account, but there are other ways your job can help you save money. Make sure you know what financial perks and discounts you can get through your job and use the ones that are valuable to you. Now, don't use this as an excuse to buy things you don't need. Just because you get a discount on retail products doesn't mean you ball out to buy things you wouldn't have bought otherwise. But if, for example, you get a corporate rate for a gym membership you would have used anyway, use those perks and save your coins.

The goal is to make sure that you're not working backward. If every penny you earn is being sucked away into debt, and you're constantly feeling the weight of trying to look like you're balling when you're not, you're going to stay stuck, no matter how much money you make. If you've got a corporate job, you've got the good fortune of having a regular paycheck. Don't waste that privilege. Make sure you're approaching your money right, saving as much as you can afford to, and getting the most bang for your buck wherever you can.

Andrew

A lot of people get hype about entrepreneurship, but they don't really get how much of an uphill battle it is compared to corporate life, especially when it comes to money. Pauleanna's story about being broke is way too familiar. But I definitely knew what it was like to be broke. After living in my car and on friends' couches and not knowing how I was going to pay for my education, I'm really familiar with the broke and struggling life. It's not a place I'm ever trying to be again.

I started early. I paid attention to the needs around me, watched how people consumed services, and got into little businesses and gigs that helped me make ends meet early on, like my mobile barbering business and DJing. But for a lot of people, there's no time to hope that a side hustle or business idea is going to turn a profit fast enough. Not when the landlord, the bill collectors, and Sallie Mae are all calling at once.

This is one of the huge upsides of a corporate job. If you need money now—and most people do—that steady paycheck is a blessing. I would have probably been able to move out of my car faster and skip Marine boot camp altogether if I had a corporate salary while I was struggling in college, even short term. I know it kept me out of hot water financially after graduation to have a 9-to-5 for a little bit (I'm gonna say more on that later).

Whether you're a new grad just trying to get your money right until you can create your dream business later on, or you're working on becoming the best corporate career man or woman in your industry, you should take advantage of the financial perks that come with having a corporate job right now. And to be honest, start learning how to appreciate shit in your life. It's always a perspective game, and if you can't be happy now with what you have, you will never be. You will always want more even when you have more. This is the truth, you don't have to listen to me, and most won't, but you'll realize it sooner than later as this seed in your head gets planted and grows in the next few years.

Your first investor is called Mrs. Corporate America.

A corporate salary means you know exactly what you're going to make every time you get paid. That means that once you figure out what you need to pay for—and I mean needs like rent and food, not wants like kicks and dining out—you can also come up with a regular savings plan. Take full advantage and save aggressively now. It doesn't matter if you're saving to start a business, pay for a vacation, or fatten your emergency fund, save up while you have a job and you know for sure money is coming in. If life ever throws you a financial curve ball, you'll be ready. This is also a numbers game and guess what, extreme effort = extreme results. Most "experts" say you should save 10%. I say you should save 90%. That's how opposite I am. You think I'm successful because I play by the same rules as the rest of the world? Please. This is the stuff I do behind closed doors so I can make strides when it's time for me to execute or strike. If you don't do it, accept and understand that I am where I am because I did what you won't do.

Paid to work, paid to learn = WIN-WIN

Not every business pays for bachelors and masters degrees, but some do. Find out if your employer has any programs that either fully or partially pay for their employees to upgrade their education. If they do, get on it. Even if it means going to school part-time or taking evening classes, don't waste an opportunity to get a degree without the ball and chain of student loans. Even if your workplace doesn't have an education funding program, you can still learn on their dime. Your employer likely has connects on industry conferences, and they may even offer free courses relevant to your field. If you're not sure if these exist, knock on your manager's door next time you're in the office and find out.

Get your money together for when it's time to quit the grind.

I'm talking about retirement. Unless you're planning to work until you're old and grey, you probably hope to retire at some point. Which means you're going to need a retirement savings plan. Thankfully, a lot of businesses offer these to their employees and contribute to them regularly. A little bit of your regular paycheck goes toward that too. But it's definitely a little bit. If you have extra cash left over after you worked out your budget, funnel some of that cash into your retirement plan. Your 65-year-old self will thank you.

Prepare for the worst.

If you've been paying any attention to American politics, you know health insurance is a tricky issue right now. People are either paying wild amounts for insurance or just going without it at all. A good job with a decent benefits plan is going to spare you that headache. Most benefits packages include health, life and disability insurance, major keys if you don't want to be drowning in medical bills if you end up getting really sick.

Get paid even when you're not in the office.

As an entrepreneur, especially in the early stages, taking vacations and getting sick are luxuries. Because every dollar you earn comes from you putting in work. If you're not there, you may not make money. Hard to enjoy a drink on the beach, or even a sick day in bed, when you're worried your absence is killing your bottom line. In a corporate job, you don't have to "eat what you kill" because you're not being paid for business development, productivity, or an entire system. You're just one piece of it.

Make good use of extra cash.

Day jobs often come with extra cash now and then that can work for you if you use it right. I'm talking about things like quarterly or holiday bonuses. And if you work in sales, you probably also earn commission. If you're already living well on your regular salary, don't blow your bonus at the mall on more shit you don't need. Put those extra dollars to work for you either in a savings account, your investment portfolio, or a purchase that helps you get closer to your goals.

Look, even if your job is not ideal, or a 9-to-5 isn't what you're looking for, I've just given you six financial reasons to make it work for you until you're in a place to do something else. I know I've said this about a hundred times already, and I'm probably going to say it a hundred more, but perspective is everything. See your job as an opportunity and resource to set yourself up for the future instead of just a daily grind. You're rushing like you're not going to live past 60 years old. That's 40 years past your 20s. You haven't even lived half of that yet! The yolo mindset is stupid, watch you end up dolo because all your care about is the now. Remember, you can make anything work for you if you ask the right questions and make the smartest moves. Warren Buffett said it best: it will take ten years to build a brand/business and one moment to lose it all. Be wise, be careful. If that sounds boring to you, reprogram and learn how to enjoy simple things. Or you can continue to be reckless and learn the hard way later. Your choice.

Chapter 11:
The Middle Ground

LESS WAIT. MORE WORK

Pauleanna

I've been juggling a corporate 9-to-5 with my side hustle for years now. Currently, I work as an executive assistant to four senior vice presidents at a major Canadian retailer. It's a demanding job with a busy schedule, and it challenges me every day, but I genuinely love my job. I'm also running three businesses—my personal brand, my mentorship program, and a ghostwriting firm. And I've got a fourth business in the works. Bruh, I'm busy, all the time. But somehow, I make every 24 hours count and thrive in my full-time gig while growing my businesses. This juggling act is hard, but it's not impossible. It's probably one of the craziest ninja moves I've pulled, but I make it work.

That's why I hate when people use the excuse "lack of time." Lack of time is not your issue, the inability to manage it is. People who value themselves allocate their time carefully and give a lot of thought to the way they use it. There are tons of ways to budget your time. One of my faves is Michael Hyatt's "Ideal Week" strategy.

Because time is money, you better watch how you spend it.

Just like you would with your finances, you budget out your time. You map out your week in an Excel spreadsheet or table and assign every day a theme (like planning on Fridays). Then the day is divided into different focus areas (like self-development in the morning and family time in the evening). You can also note which items are directly related to your goals and those that aren't. It's not a perfect system because life is unpredictable and even the best schedules get thrown off, but this visual representation of your week gives you a path to follow and an outline to keep you on track.

This is just one of the many ways I make the absolute most of my time. I have way too much on my plate to be slacking off and wasting hours. I try to make every minute that I'm awake count, starting with my mornings.

Wipe the sleep out of your eyes and get to business early.

I'm personally on #teamnosleep. I realize the importance of sleep to success, but I'm one of those people who can get more out of fewer hours than most people. I average about four hours a night, six on a good one. My alarm goes off at 4:30 every morning. I've been doing this for over a decade. While most people are still drooling into their pillows, I'm getting started on my to-do list. I practice the five-before-eight rule and try to cross at least five things off my to-do list before 8:00 am. During my journalism days, those early hours were spent writing articles on the train on the way into my 9-to-5 or reviewing my pieces before I sent them in. I got into the office early so I could squeeze in some writing before I started my shift.

Maybe 4:30 am is too early for you, and that's cool. But consider waking up half an hour earlier this week, and maybe an hour earlier the week after that. Start training yourself to get up earlier, and when the alarm goes off, get moving. I know it's hard, but you have to push past tired if you're going to make those early morning hours worth it. Because once your day is in full swing, it gets harder to stretch your time out. But that doesn't mean it's impossible.

When your job gets slow, side hustle fast.

Your day job is probably busy, but if there's downtime, put it to use. Slow in the office? Perfect. Get your notebook out and brainstorm, or review the plan you started the night before. Update your social media calendar or send an email or two. Those are all things you can do in 20-30 minutes of office downtime. You'd be amazed how much you can get out of those sessions.

I know because those sessions helped me write my book. While I was penning Everything I Couldn't Tell My Mother, I was working as a receptionist at a design firm. Working at the front desk had its perks. With little to no traffic coming through the office, I took advantage of the downtime to write. Not that I wasn't writing outside of work. I was pouring hours into writing after work and before, but I loved my passion so much, I literally couldn't breathe during the day without sneaking in some extra time. During slow periods, I'd pull out my notebook and handwrite my story, so I could go home and type it up.

Of course, if your boss doesn't make allowances for working on company time, don't go jeopardizing your job. But you get at least 30 minutes to an hour that is entirely yours. Yeah, I'm talking about lunchtime.

While you feed your stomach, give your passion a little something too.

I used to drive my co-workers crazy because my lunchtimes were dedicated to practicing my speeches. Because of that, I've had to decline more lunch dates than I can count. If you wanted to find me at lunchtime, your best bet was to check the empty offices and vacant boardrooms. That's where I would tuck myself away, the door closed, and walk around reciting my speech as if I was on stage in front of thousands. Use your lunch hour to get some work done too. Schedule calls or interviews, clean up your inbox, or anything else that you may need to get done during business hours.

But there's one period of time that you can stretch like no other.

Your vacation days let you take your side-hustle full time.

At least for a week or two. I legit cannot remember the last time I booked a vacation just to chill. When I go on vaca, I'm usually traveling for business – conferences, events, meetings. When I was hired by a Canadian organization to host a week-long event for millennials, I used my vacation. The time I had to go see one of my (personal) clients in Philly for a 1-day trip, I used my vacation. The time I had to go see my new agent out in New York, I used my vacation.

You can book vacations and lay on the beach the whole time. Or you can use your vacations to spend time building your hustle, expanding your network, securing new clients, or taking new opportunities. Yeah, it sucks that you can't have sun and sand right now, but skipping those experiences so you can secure the bag will let you take totally stress-free vacas when your side-hustle is a booming business.

You can't make more time, but if you're smart about it, you can stretch the time you do have by making the most of the free hours in your schedule. You've got all the hours between getting off work and going to sleep, waking up and getting to work, lunch breaks, downtime, and vacation days. You can use them to chill, or you can use them to boss up. But while you're maximizing your time, make sure you're protecting it too. Over my years as an executive assistant, I've been able to see firsthand how big bosses make sure none of their time is wasted. I've noticed four common habits that you need to pick up as you juggle your 9-to-5 and your side-hustle:

No is a word to be tossed out like confetti.

I've been copied on zillions of confidential emails. I know many company secrets and have been in rooms for the most private conversations. What I've observed is the power having a firm opinion and not backing down if you think the situation calls for it. Use your discernment and determine what things you have to do and which things you can decline (like those lunch dates I turned down to practice my speeches). And learn to say no without explaining yourself. All the times you say no to things you don't need to be doing gives you a chance to say yes to doing the things that really matter.

You're the boss, so do things your own way.

Sometimes, doing things the way they've always been done is the very reason results stay the same. Don't limit your possibilities. Staying open and exploring new ways of doing things can help you discover more efficient processes. Bam, saved time!

No agenda, no meeting.

The higher you climb in your business, and the more known you become, the more requests people are going to have to meet with you. People will always try to book time in your calendar not knowing that highly productive people are very careful about how they spend their time. Limit meetings and keep them as short as possible. Always inquire about the agenda of the meeting, because the truth is, most meetings don't need to happen. Knowing the agenda will help you determine if the hour-long meeting someone is trying to book with you can be handled in an email exchange instead.

Hesitation is deadly. Make a decision.

When I say hesitation, I don't mean careful consideration. Being decisive doesn't mean being impulsive. But once you weigh your options, you have to be decisive. Hesitation and overthinking are sure-fire ways to kill time. The hours, days, weeks, and months you spend wavering over decisions, are hours, days, weeks, and months you're not spending making things happen. I have a simple rule I go by when I'm trying to make a yes/no decision: If it's not an absolute yes, it's a hell no.

Take control of your time and your schedule and watch how much your day opens. You have time. Stretch it, maximize it, protect it, and use it to your advantage. We'll hit you with some dope productivity hacks and time management tips that will help you execute the balance it takes to make the best of your time. Don't get it twisted. Those hacks and tips won't make things a breeze. Even with all the advice in the world, it's going to be a challenge. It's called making sacrifices.

You will get tired. You will have to say no to friends. You will be frustrated. But in the end, it's worth it.

Andrew

I'm a workaholic. I will literally grind till I drop. (Not suggested, by the way. I'm like Will Smith on the treadmill analogy.) When I started the O Agency, I didn't just make use of the time outside of my 9-to-5, I maxed out every minute that I wasn't at my job. That meant sleeping barely a few hours every night. I ate ramen noodles because they're cheap and they cook fast. I chugged back energy drinks so the caffeine would keep me wired and awake. You'd never find me in a gym because ain't nobody had time for that. If I was awake and not at my corporate job, I was working on getting my brand off the ground. I was willing to give up everything to make that happen. I was legit prepared to die for this dream. I was so serious, I wrote a will in case I did die before my 30th birthday because I knew the way I was working wasn't healthy.

Now that I'm starting to see some of the success I was grinding for, I've taken a step back from that craziness. I still work insane hours, but I'm taking time to focus on my health. I've hired a trainer and a cook. I'm taking time to slow down because the foundation is laid. But if I could go back in time, I wouldn't change a thing because you can't have it all, not initially at least. I pushed myself to my limits at a time when I was in the best condition to handle it. (At 21 and 22, your body bounces back from a lot of things that it won't tolerate at 30.) And I regret nothing.

But I don't tell you this story to encourage you to follow in my footsteps. I really wouldn't recommend working like that to anyone. I realize it was actually crazy and dangerous. I want y'all to thrive and have the businesses you dream of, but I don't want you to die trying to get there. Yes, you have to push it, but there are ways to make that happen that don't involve ridiculous amounts of caffeine and ramen.

Decide what's actually doable for you but understand extreme effort = extreme results, average effort = average results.

When you decide you're going to side hustle, you have to know what you have to give. Can you run on five hours of sleep every night? Can you live with working seven days straight every week? Do you want to go full-time in six months, a year, or two? How much work can you really get done in one evening or weekend? Once you've got the answers to those questions, you can set goals according to your limits that you can actually get done. Be mindful, though, that we tend to let ourselves down a lot quicker than someone else. We tend to only use 10% of our brain power and quit before we're totally empty. Although everyone is different, I do believe everyone can push a little harder with the right accountability. My encouragement to you is to push your limits a little and make your goals just a bit bigger. You want to be realistic, but you still need to be challenged. This is the definition of "be comfortable being uncomfortable." A lot easier said than done.

Once you're clear on your goals and limits, decide when you're going to work on your side-hustle.

Make your side-hustle time non-negotiable.

You have to be as committed to your side hustle as you are to your day job. The reason why most people never get their business to where they want is that you're more likely not to show up when you're the only person you have to answer to. At your job, you don't just no-show. If your schedule is 9-to-5, you show up because you have to be there or you're going to get fired. If this is really the dream and you want it to succeed, you have to make it a priority, and you have to honestly be obsessed with your goals. So, choose your side-hustle hours, block them off on your calendar, and be laser-like focused.

For people who might struggle to go all the time like I did, I came across a tip in an Inc Magazine article that might help. Melanie Deziel interviewed the creator of the Employee to Entrepreneur program, Luisa Zhou, and she suggested using the weekday evenings for smaller easier tasks and then saving harder stuff for weekends when you're fresher.

Okay, now you've got your goals and your hours, it's time to get down to work. But whatever you do, don't try to do six different things at once.

Multi-tasking doesn't make time, it splits focus.

Obviously, there are some things you can multitask—like reading during your commute as Pauleanna suggested. But you can't do more than one thing at once if those things all require you to actually pay attention. Don't let a long to-do list tempt you to try and juggle tasks. Tim Ferris says that there are only two or three things that really need to be done every day that move the needle in your business. If you get nothing else done, do those two things and fit the rest in where you can. Another nice tip is to use a sticky note, split it in half than write those two things there and do just that. For some reason, minimalism really helps from a behavioral and human nature standpoint when it comes to productivity. You can actually check out this cool app called minimiLIST, it's the bomb.

Go to bybosociety.com/productivity for a full list of productivity hacks.

Again, it's about laser-like focus. I think that's a common trait of all successful entrepreneurs. Distraction doesn't get things done. I used to do a series called "Let Go and Live" because I think it's so true. Once you let go of so many things that honestly hold you back, you get to pursue your dreams in a way that has the best chance for success. Again, me being crazy, things I let go were credit cards, my bed, my tv, living close to my family/friends, and comfort. Look, I know I'm lazy, I know I will always let myself down, so I do things in my life that force me to be focused, and that is single-handedly how I've been able to stay so consistent. It's not magic, and I'm not better than you. Because I know I'm not better than you, I just become obsessed, and naturally, I get good at what I do. Again, practical and simple mathematics.

But if you're not crazy enough to get rid of your TV and your bed, and you're struggling to stay focused, other things can help.

You can kill distraction by planning when you get to press pause.

Ever heard of the Pomodoro technique? It was invented by a dude named Francesco Cirillo in the 80s. He realized that if he tried to just work for hours without taking a break, his mind started to wander. So, he got out a timer, set it for 25 minutes, and just worked the whole time uninterrupted. Then he took a 5-minute break before diving into another 25-minute work session. The Pomodoro technique is one of those productivity hacks that comes up a lot when entrepreneurs are asked how they get things done. If you need a method like this to help you work without distraction and make sure you take breaks, you can download the Pomodoro app, or another application like Focus@Will that lets you play music during your scheduled work period, and gives you a little ding when it's time for a break.

Everyone has different circumstances, but ultimately, as Pauleanna said, we all have the same 24 hours. You have to figure out for yourself how to make them work for you, based on your life, your schedule, and how hard you're willing to push yourself. If you have to get up early, stay up late, or pass on weekend chilling, get it done.

DON'T DROP THE BALL

Pauleanna

Don't let these Instagram captions and shady tweets make you doubt yourself. You can still be poppin' with a 9-to-5. Entrepreneurship is dope, and there's so much freedom, but corporate life has its advantages too, the most obvious being a financial safety net. And with such a competitive job market, it's been a blessing to have been able to save money, start a successful business of my own and take away many lessons working with industry leaders.

Sometimes, that juggling act requires me to do some real craziness. Like the time that I left the office at 1:00 pm, hopped a flight to a conference to network with Forbes execs, slept on the floor at LaGuardia airport, flew back to Toronto on the 6:15 am, strolled into work at 8:00 am, took a bird bath at the bathroom sink, and sat down at my desk right on time like it never happened. True story. It was insane. But I made it work. I took advantage of an amazing opportunity for my writing career without compromising my corporate job.

But I haven't always been this good at the juggling act. When I was starting out as a young writer, I was so focused on succeeding at that, that I started to slack at my day job at a financial firm. I was making money and seeing some success, and I let that get to my head. When I least expected it, the president of the company pulled me into her office. She let me know that my performance wasn't cutting it. I was sitting at the reception desk every day, the first person that people met when they came into the company, and I was sleepy and distracted. So much so that people noticed and complained. They checked my computer and found that I hadn't just been half-assing it, but I had been side-hustling on the company's time.

Don't let the dream distract you and make you drop the ball.

That meeting in the president's office was one hell of a wakeup call for me. I knew I had to level up. Because I didn't hate my job. I loved it, and it provided me with incredible learning opportunities. I failed by leaving evidence that my focus was split. And there's nothing wrong with splitting your focus. Thousands of side-hustlers do it. But I was sloppy, and that posed a problem for my employer. I was cashing her checks, chasing a dream of my own, and messing with her bottom line. Not good.

If your day job is funding your life and your dream, you can't afford to be subpar. While you're on the clock, your employer's duties come first. They're not paying you to work on your dream. Like we said earlier, you can, and you should maximize your downtime at work, but don't overstep.

Sometimes, something is going to have to give.

And it can't be the job that's paying the bills. If you're struggling to keep all the balls in the air, you may have to put one down. There's no shame in slowing down on your side hustle if you're at an especially busy time in your day job, or if you're dealing with other issues. Slowing down and stepping back doesn't mean you're quitting. You're just recognizing that you're human and can only do so much at any given time.

Earlier this year, I took a little break from the blogging. I've been a blogger since 2009, and I've been consistent. Now and then, there would be a lull, but for the most part, I was pushing out posts regularly. But I always have a lot on my plate. And because I've burned out before, I know it's important to put something down now and then. This time around I chose a part of my personal brand—my blog. The world didn't end, my empire didn't collapse, and my 9-to-5 is good too.

I understand that there are times when the side hustle can't wait. I've been there. If you're in a crucial place in your entrepreneurial journey and you can't afford to quit your 9-to-5, you have to be prepared to make other sacrifices.

Get ready for the all-nighters.

I've already told you about the crazy times I've gone without sleep to make magic happen in my side hustle. As I said, I do understand a lot of people can't function well without getting their eight hours every night. But if you're the kind of person who can get things done even when you're tired, give up a little sleep so you can make sure you're checking all the items off both your corporate and entrepreneurial to-do lists. Get up early, push back your bedtime, and get familiar with power naps.

Put chill sessions on the back burner.

My social life isn't much to talk about. I always make time for special occasions such as birthdays, baby showers, weddings, and that sort of thing. But casual hangouts and Netflix and chill? Nah. Because I don't always get time between 9-to-5 to work on my side hustles, my evenings and weekends are sacred time. I do believe in coming up for air every once in a while, but when there's work to do, the choice is pretty easy. Hustle now so you can chill later.

Whatever you do to make your juggling act work, make sure you're taking care of yourself. If you're a tired, stressed out mess, you'll drop the ball at work and in other areas of your life that matter. So, if you're giving up sleep, make sure you're taking time just to relax now and then, even if it's just a spa day or sleeping in for an extra hour. If you're sacrificing your social life, remember that relationships are still important and that you need to make time for the people in your life. Sacrifice should be rewarded, just don't overdo it.

Andrew

When Pauleanna told me the story about getting called into her manager's office, I knew exactly what she meant. I had a really similar meeting myself. Because you can only be checked out so long before people start to notice. It shows in your demeanor and your attitude, but most importantly, it shows in your work. When I started to lose interest at Pepsi, my manager was not impressed, and I found myself sitting in his office wondering if I was going to be fired.

But he just asked me, "Do you even want to be here? Because there are people out there who want this job."

Talk about a wake-up call. I knew I had a decision to make. Stay and put in work, or quit. I couldn't keep showing up halfway. It wasn't good for the company, and it didn't look good on me. I know I have a ridiculous work ethic, but if I got fired from a corporate job for poor performance, it would have been tough trying to convince other people I wanted to work with that I wasn't a slacker.

So, I took my mentor's advice, and I went back to work and did the right thing. I showed up, I focused, and I gave my all. That's what I had committed to do when I signed the job contract and accepted the relocation bonus. They were keeping up their end of the bargain—my paycheck never bounced. So, I had to get it together and do my part too.

I realize that Pauleanna and I aren't special cases. I mean, people who have a passion outside their day jobs are gonna struggle to stay focused and committed when all they want is to be working on their dream. I hear it all the time when new entrepreneurs message me and tell me they're falling off at work because they just don't want to be there anymore. I don't judge them because I know the struggle is real. But I also know the struggle isn't an excuse.

Passion isn't an excuse to rob your employer.

When I get those messages from side-hustlers who want to quit, I ask them if they'd just steal money from someone. Sounds extreme but, I mean, that's what we did, right? Me and Pauleanna, and all the distracted entrepreneurs I talk with. Whether we show up to work and we're half-assing it, or we're sneaking in work on the company's time, we're basically stealing money from them. Because we're not being productive. We're not giving them the level of work they're paying us for. And if we're really distracted, we could literally be messing with their bottom line. So, basically, we're dropping the ball on our end and taking their money anyway. Would you want that if this was your company?

If you're struggling to stay focused and dedicated at work, you need to get it together. If you're giving them less than your best, less than the thing they hired you for, you're stealing from the company. Don't convince yourself that your little part won't matter. It does. On some scale, your slacking is costing your boss money. Doesn't matter if it's just a few dollars, it's a matter of right and wrong. If you're planning on one day owning a business of your own, you're going to want your employees to come correct every day, so you gotta do it too.

There's absolutely nothing wrong with side hustle culture, and I'm glad that it's growing. But I don't think people are careful enough about how they execute it. People start side hustles all the time and not enough of them think about how that connects to their employment. I'm not just talking about distraction, though I've explained how important that is. But people also need to make sure that when they start their 5:00 pm - 9:00 am businesses that they're not breaching any part of the contract they signed when the got hired at their 9-to-5.

Don't side hustle your way into a firing because you're breaching your terms of hire.

Find the contract you signed and read it over. Find the employee code of conduct too. Make sure there aren't any rules about employees starting businesses outside of the company. If you can't find anything, ask questions. Keep them hypothetical. You don't want to get yourself fired because you spilled the beans to the wrong person. But you need to find out if the company has an official or unofficial policy on side hustling so that you don't find yourself screwed or sued. Also, be mad careful if you're doing a side hustle that's related to what you do at your 9-to-5. The last thing you want is to end up in court over proprietary information. Big companies have budgets for lawyers and time for court, and you could end up with a lawsuit on your hands, or your business and everything you developed under it might end up getting seized by your employer.

If you find out your good to go with your business, and your boss doesn't mind if you squeeze in some side hustling on lunch breaks while you're in the office, don't get too comfortable. As tempting as it might be to print that 45-page document on the company printer—because printer ink is mad expensive—you probably shouldn't.

Your employer's resources aren't yours to just use however you like.

That's stealing too. Well, they'd call it something like "misuse of company resources" right before they fire you. But I'm calling it what it is. You can't just use the resources they purchased to operate their business to handle yours. Printing, computer use, stationery—all of that belongs to your employer. So, use it for your employer.

I feel like I've talked about a lot of don'ts, but there's one thing you definitely should do. Get a calendar that consolidates your 9-to-5 commitments with your side-hustle tasks.

One calendar for both jobs makes sure you never double-book.

Whether you use an app like Google Calendar or the calendar app on your phone, or you do things the old fashion way with a wall calendar or a day planner, make sure you note down all your due dates for both jobs. This way, you never book side-hustle work when you have big deadlines for your 9-to-5, and you'll never drop the ball. Plus, it will make it so much easier for you to see where your free time is and then you can fit your brands work into it.

Whatever you do, make sure you don't step on your employer's toes and just don't drop the ball. You absolutely can be committed to building an amazing brand without leaving your boss hanging or getting yourself fired. Just make sure you cover your bases, respect the contracts you signed, and keep it honest.

AUTOMATE, DELEGATE, ELIMINATE

Andrew

Productivity is all about how you use your time. You have to decide what tasks need to be done right now, which ones can wait, which ones you should pass off to somebody or something else, and which ones can be thrown out. Back in the day, I used "Do, Don't Delegate, and Delay" or the 4Ds. Every morning, I'd get up and look at my to-do list and decide which items fit into what category. By the time I started my day, I'd have cut the list of things I actually had to do myself down, because the rest I either assigned to someone else, pushed to another day, or decided to just cut from the list altogether. I can't remember where I first learned it, but there are a few variations of the concept.

One that I really like now is Rory Vaden's Focus Funnel. Every task goes through a funnel of assessment—Eliminate, Delegate, Automate, Concentrate and Procrastinate. If you can't get rid of the task, you figure out if you can pass it on. If it can't be passed on, you decide if you can use an app, program or system to automate it. If you can't automate it, then you know the task is yours to do, and you just have to decide if you need to do it right now, or if it can wait.

It's not extremely different from the 4Ds, except for one key thing: automate.

Automation lets you pull time out of thin air.

Well, not exactly but it's pretty damn close. Automation is legit one of my favorite business terms. If you're not on top of current business software and technology used to automate processes that will save you time and cut costs, you're probably moving too damn slow and spending too damn much. Seriously, catch up. You have to be on top of the applications and software that work best and will help you move your business forward.

I've spent the last five years and almost $75,000 discovering and testing the best systems and processes and hacks to apply to my own business at the O Agency. The amount of time automation has freed up, and how efficient it's made me and my team, I'd say that money is well worth it.

There are parts of my business that can operate without me or my team touching them. This is so important if you're going to keep your 9-to-5 while you build your brand, and especially if your boss isn't cool with you using any company time to do work of your own. If you take a little bit of time to set these things up in advance, you can save yourself hours of extra labor and have things done exactly when you want them. So, I'm going to let you in on some of my faves.

Kill it on social media without ever opening the apps.

If you spend an hour setting up your social media for the week on Sunday, there are apps that will auto-post your tweets and Facebook, LinkedIn and Google posts for you. Instagram was late to the party, but you can now post to your IG via Hootsuite. That means if you're running social media campaigns, promotional content, or sharing links, you don't have to remember to pull your phone out or risk messing up your carefully scheduled campaigns. Buffer and Hootsuite are both well known and reliable, and they both allow you to handle multiple accounts across several brands. They're great because you can see all your accounts in one place, plus they give you analytics that can help you create smarter campaigns and content your audience is actually interested in.

Handle all your money moves, both in and out.

Accounting can be a real pain because it's so time-consuming. But there are some great automation tools that make it way easier. If you have expenses or invoices that recur monthly, weekly, or daily, you can use a tool like Freshbooks, Waveapps, or Due that you can set and forget unless something changes.

Master your inbox. And your customers' inboxes too.

Emails eat time, I swear. But there are some email automation tips and tools that can help you cut back on the time you spend in your emails while still making sure you land in your clients' inboxes when you want to. For example, if there are certain types of emails you send all the time, you can set up templates in Gmail and Outlook. Next time you need to contact a client with one of your standard messages, you can just select it from the list, it'll populate the client's name, and you can just hit send. For email newsletters, MailChimp and Constant Contact are cool. They've got a wide range of templates, let you set up different mailing lists, and allow you to track opens, click-throughs, and other analytics. Hatchbuck is also dope for email marketing because not only does it send out your campaign, but it allows for automated follow-ups that can help keep sales from slipping through the cracks.

Schedule meetings without ever having to make a call or send an email.

If you regularly have phone or video chat meetings with clients, but you don't want to go through the hassle of setting them up all the time, there are tools that let you share your availability, so clients can choose the time that works for them too. Check out Calendly which is perfect for setting up one-on-ones and links to your Google Calendar, so you'll know exactly when you're booked. And Doodle takes all the hassle out of trying to figure out what time works for your whole team. Everyone just shares their availability, and you set up your meeting for a time when everyone overlaps.

These are just some of the amazing tools that can help you automate key parts of your business so you can focus on the things that only you can do. These tools range in price from free to kinda pricey, but time is money, and the investment is well worth it. If you're looking for more, we'll be creating and updating a list of the best business tools on the BYOB Society website, including more of our favorite automation apps and sites.

Pauleana

Delegate. Delegate. Delegate.

That's my winning secret to getting through each day. I have a ton on my plate. I'm not complaining about it. But the reality is it's too much for me to do on my own. So, when people ask me how I conquer my goals and get things done, I keep it very real: this is not a one-woman show. There's a monster of a team standing behind me working very hard every single day. At some point, you have to let others lead you in areas of your weakness. When you move from solopreneurship to having a team of staff or interns, you get to multiply yourself freeing up your time to do what you do best and leave the rest to the people you hired to do the other stuff.

For me, it started with one woman. My assistant, Desiree. Working as an assistant to high-level executives, I quickly learned how valuable it was to have a right-hand person who can make sure certain things run smoothly while you handle what you do best. A few years back, I put out a request on Facebook for a part-time assistant. Desiree was one of the first of many ladies who slid into my inbox with a killer resume. She was essential to helping me keep my business running. Des helped me organize my to-do list, figure out what tasks I needed to address most urgently, followed up on my emails, managed my calendars, and took care of travel, meeting and event arrangements. While she took care of those things, I was able to focus on the things I did best.

Des has since gone on to start her own event coordination business (so proud of her), and I had Chelsea and Patricia who both took over the reigns. Chelsea has since moved on to start her own platform (super cool) and Patricia is still by my side and doing an amazing job keeping me on track. She's now one of over 20 team members and freelancers across my three brands, including a publicist, videographer, website designer, social media consultant, a team of talented writers and more. Each person brings a refreshing perspective to the table and inspires the heck out of me too.

Magic happens when you build a team you can trust with your baby.

Even if it's just a team of one. I chose every single person on my team because, like me, they have an insane amount of work ethic, they're innovative and take initiative, and they know how to be flexible to get things done. And that's why I can trust them. My staff helps me run the ship while I am out on the ground learning and developing a game plan for us to grow. They pull all-nighters, they contribute brilliant ideas, and I can trust when something needs to get done, it will get done. And that changed the game because a good team opens your world right up.

You can breathe. Really breathe. My team has allowed me to take breaks with less anxiety. Before I built my team, I couldn't imagine taking a vacation without my laptop. I just wouldn't have had the time, and I would have spent the entire vaca stressing. To be honest, I still haven't taken a work-free vacation. But now, that's by choice. I can if I want to because I know things will run even if I step back for a while.

While I haven't caught a flight to the islands yet, I have been able to take up other awesome opportunities I would have had to pass up if my team wasn't there. Before my team, there were so many exciting projects that would come across my desk that I had to say no to. It was so annoying, but I literally had no capacity. Like two years ago, when I was invited to Nigeria to speak at a conference, I had to turn it down. And it hurt because I had been praying so hard for my first speech across the world, but I couldn't drop what I already had on the go. Now, I'm able to say yes to more because I have more hands. My team let me make space for the new.

Of course, despite having an awesome team, there's still a lot I have to make sure I take care of. My to-do list is always long. So, it's really important for me to take that list and make sure I tackle it in the way that makes the most sense.

To-do lists need to be based on what matters most.

When you're the boss, everything is 'urgent.' You have to learn what needs your attention right this second and what can wait. It's critical to set timelines and objectives at the beginning of each day. Get the most important things done first, the things that cannot wait until tomorrow or the things that will make tomorrow easier. Yes, your inbox can wait. You don't have to respond immediately to every single email you get. I have four email accounts. If I answered every email right away, I would honestly be spending my entire day replying to clients, friends, and colleagues. Listen, just because they think it's urgent, doesn't mean you need to push their request to the top of your list. Prioritize your tasks and then execute.

The best way to execute is to kill distraction.

Yes, kill it and bury it. Our world is full of distractions. Whether it's social media, crappy TV, invites to parties, or the things towards the bottom of the to-do list, those things can't get in the way of you taking care of the task at hand. You need to learn how to say no before distractions get the best of you. For instance, I am such a sucker for reality television, so just like Andrew, I got rid of my TV. I replaced it with a desk. Yes, you heard me. I replaced my lovely big screen with a desk so I can focus without being drawn into the Kardashian household or tempted by Real Housewives of ATL drama. It also helps to make a part of your day "communication-free." If there are tasks you can't afford to split your attention on, this is the time to do them. No cell phone, no social media, no visitors, nothing. Focus gets things done.

Put yourself on your to-do list.

You can delegate and prioritize all you want, but none of that will matter if you're burned out. The only person who can take care of you is you, so make time for that. It's okay to take a time-out to collect your thoughts. Take care of you first and foremost because it's key to your productivity. To avoid feeling like I'm part of a circus and keep myself from burning out, I make time for one thing a day that is important to me that doesn't involve my computer or phone. Whether that's a dip in my jacuzzi, taking myself out for a lunch date to my favorite restaurant, or getting in a home workout, I make time to do things that are good for me, so I'll have the energy to do everything else on the list.

The point here is not only to exercise better time management practices so that you can get the most out of your day, but to also take better care of you. You are no good to anyone if you constantly feel overwhelmed or you are on the verge of a breakdown. All the time in the world is useless if you can't use it.

Chapter 12:
Time That Jump Just Right

SILENCE YOUR IMPULSIVE SIDE

Andrew

If you're riding that line between 9-to-5 and side hustle, the urge to jump can be unbearable. When you spend the hours between 5:00 pm and 9:00 am building something you really love and believe in, it gets hard to want to show up for anything else. You want to give your every waking minute to that thing. Doing anything else feels like a waste. I can't tell you how many times during my first month at Pepsi I woke up and thought, "Man, I could just stay home today and do something for my brand."

And I could have made the leap, financially. Between my corporate job, my DJ gigs, and my clients at the O Agency, I was pulling in just a little under $100,000 every year. It may have been shaky if things went sideways with my business, but I had a decent cushion. But it wasn't time. No matter how excited I was, I couldn't move before the time was right because excitement and hope don't keep businesses afloat.

So, when I say silence that impulse that's telling you to jump before you're really prepared, I mean it. Being able to pace yourself and stay humble is a sign of maturity. Don't get caught up in those stories of entrepreneurs who dropped everything with $10 to their name, maxed out 12 credit cards and hustled till they made it convince you that you gotta rush and just handle the struggle that comes with moving too fast.

Don't set yourself up to fail.

Because for every one of those "inspiring" stories, there are about nine businesses that just failed. I'm talking bankruptcy-type failure. That's not a number I just made up either. Statistics show that 90% of startups fail. And there's no real way to guarantee you'll be a part of the 10%, but you can definitely set yourself up for failure if you get too caught up in these success stories about jumping all in before you're really ready for everything that comes with entrepreneurship.

There's no sense in pre-fabricating struggle. I get that some people can deal with having their back against the wall financially. That's cool. In fact, it's important, because as an entrepreneur, a time may come when you have to crawl back from a deficit. But don't allow yourself to be in that position for lack of trying. Don't leap when you're broke. There's no sense in quitting your job just to put your back up against the wall, thinking it will push you to get things together fast. Because prefabricated struggle doesn't elicit the same reaction as a real rough break.

I know you want to be a full-time entrepreneur. Good, that drive is important. But you gotta realize how good you've got it when you still have a day job. Because the minute you stop "working for the man" and start working for yourself, you're going to realize that you barely understood what working hard is. When you walk away from your 9-to-5, there's no safety net except the one you set up. So, make sure you know your business can sustain itself and keep you fed before you leap, no matter what your impulses say.

And don't let side hustle slander make decisions for you.

You've got to tune out people who are telling you to jump when they're not assuming any of the risks that come if you fall. You wouldn't believe the amount of crazy successful businesses that started out as side hustles and didn't become main gigs until the founders were sure that was the best move. Let me give you some examples.

The creator of Minecraft, the most popular computer game of all time, Markus Persson, released the game in 2009 but didn't go full-time for a year. He sold Minecraft to Microsoft in 2014 for $2.5 billion.

Steve Wozniak and Steve Jobs invented the Apple computer while still working their day jobs. Wozniak was at Hewlett-Packard, and he tried to offer the design to his employer five times, but they said no every time. Jobs worked with Atari and invited the CEO to invest. I don't have to tell you how big they are now.

Phil Knight spent six years working a day job as an accountant while he sold running shoes at night. The brand he built? Nike, one of the most well-known sneaker companies to ever exist. It's worth 25 billion dollars.

Instagram started as a side hustle in 2010. Kevin Systrom and Mike Krieger started the social platform together, working at a desk they rented in a shared office space on evenings and weekends. They sold Instagram to Facebook in 2012 for a billion dollars.

That's just four out of hundreds of examples of amazing businesses and brands that started out as side hustles and grew into million- and billion-dollar businesses. Their founders didn't rush into full-time entrepreneurship. They built something solid before leaving their day jobs behind.

Ideally, you want to out-earn your day job before you quit.

You shouldn't hand in your resignation until it costs you money to step away from your business to go to your day job. I like how Mark J. Kohler put it. "Do the math. Make sure your business can afford you and the day job has a tangible cost that you can calculate. Don't just quit the day job because it feels like the right thing to do. Make sure you run the numbers and then run them again. It's not worth the risk."

But that's the ideal situation. I understand if you want to make the move earlier. And realistically, I think it's possible for any entrepreneur to quit their job in two years with the right action plan. The first thing you need to do is make quitting your end goal, and then put the steps in place to get there.

Start by saving your safety net.

Most businesses start out with a $20,000 investment. If you're going to quit in two years, you'll need to save $10,000 of your yearly income each year and live on the remainder of your earnings. Of course, that's going to take some sacrifices. When I was preparing to quit Pepsi, and into the first few years of entrepreneurship, I learned to live way below my means. I found low-cost housing in a smaller city and paid about $700 a month in rent. I deferred my student loans, ate ramen noodles, kept the AC off, and got rid of luxuries like cable. It was tough, but I made it work because I needed to make sure that when I quit, I was going to have something to keep the bills paid. Figure out where you can cut costs so you can save the money you need to quit.

Whether you choose to wait until your business is turning a sustainable profit, or save a safety net and jump early, just make sure that you've prepared yourself for the realities of the transition. Full-time entrepreneurship is not something to take up on a whim. It's a challenging enough road. Don't create extra roadblocks for yourself by rushing in.

If you're still feeling the itch to jump before you've really done what you need to, seek advice.

Talk to somebody who's walked the walk and made it to the other side.

This is why mentors are so important. If you've got someone in your life who's already been through this, they'll be able to help you see if you're ready and keep you humble if you're getting arrogant. My mentor helped me stay on track and made sure I had everything in place before I resigned. When it was time, she gave me the nod and helped me write my resignation letter. I remember the day I handed in that letter to my boss.

The only thing I felt nervous about was telling him I was resigning because I'd never left a job before. But I was so excited to leave. I felt like I was retiring. I was able to feel that way because I knew I had done what I needed to do so I could move with confidence.

SELLING CHANGE

Andrew

Alright, you've done the prep, the bank account is stacked right, and you're just about ready to leap into full-time. Dope. You're about to make one of the biggest moves in your life. It's going to be risky. Every entrepreneurial venture is. No matter how much prep you do, there's going to be risk. But the best entrepreneurs are the ones who can minimize risk, and the best way to minimize risk is to take every precaution you can. At this point, if you've done everything you're supposed to, all the things you need should be in place, but I want to give one final checklist for you to follow to make sure you've taken all the right steps and that you've got all the tools and resources to make it out here in these entrepreneurial streets.

Make sure everything is legit.

If your business isn't registered yet, what the hell have you been waiting for? Before you make another move, incorporate your business as either an LLC or a SCorp. This is the thing that will set your business apart from the people who just have a hobby. It'll also make sure you don't get yourself in trouble with the tax man. The IRS doesn't play when it comes to taxes and neither should you.

Ditch @gmail.com and brand your company email. Even if it's just you.

Sign up for a G Suite account. It's the business version of Gmail, and it's going to make you look way more professional. For just $5/month, you'll get a branded email address (e.g. name@yourcompany.com) that will match your domain name and assure customers they're dealing with someone who's really about their business. As a bonus, G Suite comes with way more than email. You get Google Calendar, Drive, Slides, Sheets,

Forms, and a few other tools that make running your business a whole lot smoother. And as you grow, you can give employees their own email address with your domain name too so that everybody looks legit.

Set up shop, or at least look like you did.

If you're planning to have a brick and mortar shop, I'm going to go ahead and assume you already got the real estate handled. But for service-based brands, office space could be a good look, especially if you have a team or meet with clients a lot. You can rent a space in an office building or join a co-working space. Both of those can be pretty expensive, so don't rush into it if you don't need it. But even if you don't have a physical office space, you need to have a business mailing address that isn't your house. (Do you want the whole world having your home address? Yeah, didn't think so). So, you have a couple of options. You can get a PO Box with your local post office or mailing service. Tim Ferris suggests manipulating the address, so it looks like a building address. (You can use the post office street address and put your PO Box as the suite number. But be warned, this isn't standard, and your mail may get lost in the void). You can also get a virtual office location through a service like ServCorp or a digital mailroom like Nimble Mail where your mail will be sent, opened, scanned and emailed to you. You can then decide if you want to have the physical copy sent to you, and what junk mail you want to be filtered.

Get a business line so clients aren't ringing off your cell at midnight.

At some point, you're going to have to talk to clients on the phone, and you may not want it to be your cell. No matter how many times you post your business hours, people are guaranteed to call outside of them. So, if you don't want your cell phone vibrating in the wee hours of the morning with a client on the other end, a dedicated business line is a smart move. There are a few ways you can do this. You can go the traditional route and get a standard landline through a phone service provider. You can forward it to your cell phone the old school way if you don't want to miss calls while you're on the go. As a more high-tech and cheaper alternative, you could go with Google Phone which uses your Gmail address to set you up with a dedicated phone line. The number is free, local, and can be routed to any existing line you have. Plus, it's got some cool perks, like voicemail capabilities and a do not disturb feature that can help you enforce those office hours. Don't forget though, it's an internet phone service, so no WiFi/data, no phone calls.

Don't give customers an excuse to pay you late or not at all. Give 'em options.

E-transfers are cool and all until a client doesn't want to pay you that way, or they live in another country. There are a lot of good and reliable payment services out there that will help you make sure you get your coins in your account on time and with ease. Paypal is pretty much accepted anywhere and is always a good option to have. Plus, setting up a business account with them is easy. Square and Stripe are good too. Square is especially good because it lets you accept credit card payments from clients you meet with face-to-face. There are quite a few others including Google Wallet, ProPay, and Shopify. They come with various perks, transaction fees, and features, so make sure you choose one that fits your needs and budget.

While we're talking money, make sure you have an accounting app that lets you create invoices, send quotes, estimates, and receipts, and gives you access to expense reports. I mentioned WaveApps when I talked about automation, but they cover a lot of accounting functions, and it's totally free. Other popular options are Freshbooks, Quickbooks, and Xero.

Just be sure you have the tools that are going to help you run your business daily, make your clients trust that you're actually legit, and keep you making money long after you quit your 9-to-5. There are a ton of options out there for most of the essentials I've listed here. Do your research, read the reviews, and choose the one that's going to fit you best. You custom built your business, so don't be afraid to customize the things that help you keep it running.

Pauleanna

If your side hustle is booming and you're ready to trade in your 9-to-5 for a 24/7, there are just a few more things you need to get in place first. Both Andrew and I talked about the importance of not rushing into the jump before your money's right. The last thing you want to do is end up broke a few months after you go full-time with your business because you didn't put a safety net in place and didn't take steps to keep your income flowing in and not out. So, I wanted to share some strategies that will help you set yourself up financially when you go full-time.

Smart money makes money.

Sometimes, it's the simple strategies that help you keep maximize your business' income. I'm Canadian and operate all my businesses from the north side of the border, but I've got a few US clients. Because the US dollar is stronger than the Canadian, the currency exchange rate works in my favor. It's a simple (perfectly legal) chess move that changes the way I play my game. Consider smart business strategies that will help you get your money up, like developing service packages combining your different offerings, or if you have a physical product, shopping around for the most reasonably priced wholesalers.

Another smart and essential move? Get a financial advisor in your corner. If you've got financial mess, they'll help you clean it up and stay in the black as you move ahead with your business. They'll also help you strategize ways to make the most of your businesses earnings. Thanks to my financial advisor, I have a Registered Retirement Savings Plan which will be a major key when I drop my corporate gig and give up my company-funded pension. Set yourself up now so that you're not scrambling in the future.

Stress-proof your financial plan.

Even the best plans get waylaid. You may think you have your finances set up for entrepreneurship, but a single emergency can screw that up if you're not prepared. We all know that emergencies can happen at a drop of a dime, so examine your plan regularly so you can adjust it before something happens. If your goals also include things like marriage, homeownership, and children, you want to make sure your financial plan makes room for those things, even as you're building your business. These are all things you'll want to share with your financial planner so you can put a solid strategy in place to make sure you can afford the life you really want.

Use your strengths to make mo' money mo' ways.

I am all for making multiple streams of income. In fact, every single one of my business mentors has recommended it. But there's a ridiculous trend right now where people are swerving into lanes they shouldn't be in. Personally, I excel at mentoring, consulting, writing and public speaking. Those are my lanes, and I stay in them. I have no business selling services or products outside of that. You won't find me in the fitness industry or launching a clothing line. That's not my dream. Instead, I use what I'm bomb at to diversify my income. If you've got a service-based business or a product-focused brand, consider all the different ways you can offer your customers the things you do best. Consider coaching services, digital products, affiliate income, public speaking or live events. But remember, focus on what you're good at because wasted time doesn't make money.

Don't feel guilty when people can't afford you.

You're not going to take it full-time if you're making peanuts off your services. One of the big mistakes I made early on as a solo entrepreneur was that I undercharged. I had paid my dues, my work was good, clients were singing my praises, but I was burnt out because I was overworked and underpaid. If your work is up to standard, go on and raise your prices and don't let anybody guilt you about it.

And believe me, people are going to try. People will see a price they can't afford and say, "You're too expensive." Don't take it personally. What they really mean is that they cannot afford you, and that means they're no longer your target market. That's not a diss to them. That's just the facts. If you know your services are worth the price you're charging, don't let people haggle you (unless you feel inclined to offer a discount). Nicki Minaj once told a story in an interview about showing up to a video shoot early in her career, and instead of catered food, there was just a jar of pickles on a table. She was not impressed, and she spoke up for herself.

Dope author, Luvvie Ajayi, brought up that story in an interview for Forbes, and I love what she said when she was asked if she had ever been offered "pickle juice":

"All the time. As a freelancer, as a writer, and running my company, people have always tried to negotiate me down. Some might think that I might accept their offers because they think I don't have many options. The truth is, I always have options available to me. I won't allow a pickle juice precedent to be set. I know my worth."

You always have options. The market is deeper and bigger than the few clients who don't want to pay your prices. If you listen to people in the 'too expensive' camp, your side hustle will always feel like a struggle, and you'll be back at your corporate job in a blink.

Money math: don't just add, multiply.

Earning more is great, but if you can multiply those earnings, you're really talking. The first thought that comes to my mind is invest, invest, invest. All the income I made from my businesses, I put it right back in. That meant hiring staff, paying for conferences and other educational opportunities, spending money on marketing, and working with coaches who could help me sharpen my skills.

Entrepreneurship is an expensive undertaking, and with all the other stress that comes with running a business full-time, you want to do your best to make sure your financial safety net is securely in place. You can't predict everything that will happen, and chances are you may hit some financial roadblocks along the way. But if you get off on the right foot, it'll make catching yourself that much easier.

NOTES

BRANDING
FOR ENTREPRENEURS

Chapter 13:
Money Matters

THE BURDEN OF BORROWING

Andrew

There's an undeniable reality about starting a business: no matter what it is, it's going to cost you money. No matter how many free things you can find, borrow, or beg for, at some point, you're going to need to invest some cold hard cash into getting your business or brand off the ground and keeping it up. So where does the money come from?

(Side Note: you're always investing in yourself, you're just probably doing it in a very low ROI-driven way. You invest in your perception by the clothes you wear, your health by what you eat, your comfort by the rent you pay, your mind by the TV/podcasts/Netflix "entertainment" value you pay for. It makes me wonder, is it a money situation? Or are people just bad investors, looking for things that they "think" give them immediate value or an emotional return vs. real-life impact and legacy? You have to decide, but I would argue that it may not just be purely a money issue.)

When it comes to money, I look at it simply. There are three ways you can get the money you need to fund your business:

1. Investments or Bank Loans
2. Borrow from family and friends
3. Self-funding

Let's address these one-by-one because I think it's super important for you to understand how the choices you make around money for your business can make or break you. A bad financial choice, especially in the beginning can really eff you up, and I'm not trying to see any of you fail because you went after money the wrong way.

So, let's talk about investments first. I'm going to level with you right now, this is one of the hardest paths to take.

No one is going to invest in you if they're worried about buyer's remorse.

You have to realize that raising capital is like sales, and nobody is going to buy a product they feel isn't worth their money. Especially if that product is a business they have no proof is worth their money. You wouldn't go out and buy a house without seeing it first, or a car without test driving it. That's crazy, right? So why do you expect that investors are going to throw cash at you when your business is just an idea with no validation of any kind. Investors need time and proof that investing in your business makes sense. If you don't have proof, get some, or accept that you're not ready to ask big ballers for their money.

Here's another ugly reality you need to get comfortable with if you're trying to secure investors. They're hard to come by for minorities and women who don't already have big, successful businesses. And even then, it's a struggle. And don't tell me about this person or that person who got funding. You know what? They're privileged, and you're not. It sucks, but the faster you realize life isn't fair, the more focused you can be on what is important instead of looking at the outside world and assuming the same rules apply to you. I realized this early, and I adjusted and moved to the beat of my own rhythm.

It's a well-documented fact that minority and female founders are crazy underfunded. The reason why? Most investors and venture capitalists invest in people they trust, and amongst things like physical and mental prowess, trust is built on relatability and cultural identity. Think about it, when you look at someone of a similar race or creed, it's easier for you to say 'that's my brother or sister, I can feel what they're going through.' It's always a trust thing. I genuinely believe it would be the same way if the script was flipped and minorities were the ones with money to invest. Don't get mad at the reality though, use it to your advantage. Either prepare to get funding some other way, or be willing to be that token child. We all know diversity is a big dea

l and businesses are pushing for it more. If you can, be that minority token that investors choose, climb the ranks, and then put your people on. Stop crying and play the long-term game. If that's not something you're willing to do, it's time to create a Plan B.

Don't get down because you can't get money out of investors' pockets.

I feel like people hear no from investors and they let negativity take control from there. Instead of looking for solutions, they feel entitled to investment and get salty because they didn't get it. Or they get mad when someone who is less qualified gets the funding they wanted. I understand that some people who don't get funding are getting screwed when they shouldn't be, but you can't let that stop you. That mindset will mess you up. This is what your grandparents meant when they said, "Life ain't fair." It isn't, and it sucks. But the question is what are you going to do? Because there's money out there. Always remember, all it takes is one yes to get to the next level. One yes. One percent. One out of 100 nos. Drill that into your head and push past those 99 failures.

Okay, so investors are probably out. Your next option is a loan, either from the bank or from family and friends. I'm going to tell you to say no to both.

Leave bank loans alone.

One of my favorite entrepreneurs, Mark Cuban, said it's stupid to get a loan for a business. When you're starting out, there's so much uncertainty. The only certainty is that you're gonna owe a payment on the loan at the end of 30 days. That's not a tactic that eliminates risk. It's not a smart move at all. Borrowing money from the bank is always a high risk because even if you don't profit you still owe. And now you're working from a deficit. That's if you get the loan at all. Because you're not getting a good one if your "financial brand"—your credit—isn't good. If you do get a loan with bad credit, the loan is going to be a low amount with a high interest rate, and you're starting in the hole anyway.

Don't let your mama lend you money either.

Yeah, it's true that whether they give it to you as a gift or a loan, it's much easier to persuade your friends and family to believe in your business and invest a little than it is to convince investors and venture capitalists. The process is a hell of a lot easier. But I don't encourage people to take money from friends and family because it's so much more pressure. Pressure on them to trust that you're going to make their money back, and pressure on you to not fail. Starting a business comes with enough pressure as it is. You don't need the added stress of worrying that any failure will let even more people down. Plus, there's the worry of having to pay back money you didn't earn. Man, drop that where it is. So that leaves us with option #3.

Come up with the money by your damn self.

I always suggest working and saving, like I did, because it's so much easier when the only person you're at risk of letting down financially is yourself. But there's another upside to self-funding that I think most people don't realize. (We've got a great article on byobsociety.com/leanstartup with good ways to go about this!)

Self-funding ensures the slow growth that keeps your head on straight.

Most of the money that has gone into my businesses came out of my pocket. All those hours I put in at my 9-to-5 and spinning at Hampton basketball games helped me earn the cash that got the O Agency started in the early days. Damn, it was a grind. But I'm grateful for it. You know why? Because it taught me patience. And that's valuable. Slow growth is important. I know people want things fast, but it's not good. When you peak fast, you plateau early. You make bad decisions because you didn't learn the lessons that come with the climb. And when you hit your peak early, the only place to go is down. The nice thing about never peaking is that you're always going up! Even now, most people would deem me successful. I have multiple businesses and a recent feature in Gary Vee's new book. I travel, tour, speak, do cool videos and so much more. And guess what? I'm only operating at 20%, 25% max. I have so much more in me! When you have to work hard and hustle for it, your mindset and behavior are all different. It's worth the wait.

If you feel you can't self-fund, invest in some patience.

That's really the only reason why an entrepreneur wouldn't be able to start a business without an investor. Because they aren't willing to put in the time to earn the money they need. They want to get it fast, and they're willing to assume all the risk that comes with that—the high interest rates, the pressure of repayment, the chance of digging yourself into a financial hole if you make nothing and still have to come up with payments. It's a nightmare you could avoid if you're just willing to wait a little and work a lot.

"Remember this, many people think entrepreneurship is risky, however, the best entrepreneurs are simply the ones who have figured out how to minimize risk. It may look risky to the world, but behind closed doors, they've completely game planned their growth and success. It might be boring, like the Patriots and the Spurs, but they f*cking win, and that's what matters."

Don't be too discouraged, though. If self-funding feels really out of reach, there are ways to get funding that don't leave you with repayment pressure.

Get the public to believe in you enough to give you money for small rewards.

I'm talking about crowdfunding. The first big funding project I did was completely crowdfunded. My first client was my best friend, Bakari Taylor. After I helped him develop his personal training business, including logos, a business plan, and boot camp events, he got great reception, and we decided it was time to go bigger. We planned a seven-city East Coast tour and crowdfunded $10,000 on Indiegogo. It was a huge win funding-wise, but it was a marketing win too because we were able to test the interest in Bakari's brand and the idea of fitness tours.

If you're planning to do crowdfunding, there are a few things you'll want to consider:

Choose a platform that's going to give you a win no matter what.

Certain crowdfunding platforms, like Kickstarter, require you to hit your financial target to get any of the money you raise. If you set a goal of $10,000 and only make $9,990, they're hitting refund for every donor, and you get nothing. I suggest Indiegogo because you get the cash even if you miss your target.

Don't lose because you don't know how to play the marketing game.

Crowdfunding may seem simple — set your goal, tell your story, set the rewards and wait for the money to pour in — but it's way more complicated than that. If you want thousands of people to donate to your project, you're going to have to sell them on it. Find out the kind of incentives people are actually going to be interested in. Some people are going to give purely because they believe in your idea. But some people are in it for the reward, so make it something they're really going to want. Make sure you tell your story really well and mix it up. Use pictures, videos, and really good writing that's going to have people hooked on your idea. Play to the emotions. Emotional Marketing is by far one of the best ways to create certainty and convince people to buy into you because people like what feels good. And push hard on social media. If you think people are just going to stumble across your campaign, you're playing yourself. Have a social media campaign ready with influencers, affiliates, giveaways, referrals, the whole nine yards. For a full list of ways to create an effective social media campaign visit byobsociety.com/socialmediacampaign.

Get out the gate fast and don't let the excitement fall off.

Stats show that if you don't raise the first 25% of your funding goal in the first 25% of your timeline, you're not going to make your target. There's always a surge at the beginning. People are excited and down to give. But that's going to fall off. So come out hard, and make sure your marketing plan includes a strategy to keep the interest up after the first few days of excitement.

Crowdfunding is a dope option, but it takes time, and you can't do it too often. Remember that when you ask people for money for anything, you can't keep asking the audience over and over again because of Marketing Fatigue

(check out byobsociety.com/marketingfatigue for a full breakdown of this problem). Gary Vee's Jab Jab Right Hook is a great resource for understanding the importance of giving to your audience before asking them for anything. But, there are a couple of other avenues you can explore.

Go head-to-head with other entrepreneurs for the money on the table.

There are tons of pitch competitions where entrepreneurs who have mastered the art of selling their business can secure the bag and get the funding they're looking for. I say, do as many pitch competitions as possible. They're not easy money by far — they take a bit of preparation and a lot of confidence — but it's worth the effort. And think about it. If you can't win a competition against 10-12 entrepreneurs, imagine how hard it is for investment dollars against hundreds and thousands of competitors! When you put it into perspective like this and start looking at everything as a chess match, you develop the hunger and competitive spirit that is truly required in the entrepreneurship space. I've personally never pitched, but I have lots of friends who have and have seen how life-changing it was for them even if they did not win. If you're going to pitch, here are some things you'll want to do:

Keep your eyes peeled for opportunities to shoot your shot.

The more you pitch, the more you can win, so you'll want to stay on top of where the competitions are happening. Some good places to check out are business schools and incubators, entrepreneurship organizations, economic development organizations, and websites that focus on small businesses. We'll be compiling a more complete list of places to find competitions on the BYOB website, so be sure to check it out.

Do a little background check on your judges.

If you know who your judges are, you can figure out how to cater your pitch. Knowing a bit about their business background and entrepreneurship style could help you hook them and keep them at the edge of their seats, eager to hear what you have to say.

Know your ish.

Seriously, a pitch competition isn't something you want to wing unless you don't care if you lose. Make sure you have all the info judges are going to be looking for: the problem your company solves, how you solve it, your financial figures, info on your target market, how you plan to use the money if you win, and other key info. If the judges ask questions, you'd better have answers.

Package your pitch.

Yes, you better know your stuff, but how you present it matters too. You don't usually get a lot of time, so make sure you can present all your info quickly and clearly, and in a way that won't put the judges or the audience to sleep. That means no droning on for the whole time, no sloppy slideshows, and no boring and unnecessary nonsense. Keep it impactful, be different, and think outside the box, and you'll do great. If you're going to be in a pitch contest, hit me up sometime, I love watching pitches and will gladly come out to support you. I'm serious, shoot me a message at: Andrew@theOagency.com or on IG @Brandwithdrew, and I'll show up if I have time in my schedule.

There's one final source of funding I'd like you to consider if you're struggling to raise the money on your own, and that is business grants.

Just a few well-written paragraphs and a smart business idea can get you the money.

Grants are a great resource for funding. If you take the time out to carefully complete the application and persuade the judges your business deserves the money, you can walk away with thousands of dollars. The great thing about grants is they help to counter the challenge that minorities and women face with getting funding from investors. There are tons of grants that are specifically for women, minorities, and people in certain industries. With a little bit of research, you can find government-funded or privately-run grants you can apply for.

I really hope that you see that there are so many options available to you for funding that don't involve loans. I feel like I can't say it enough—getting a loan, no matter who it's from, isn't a risk worth taking unless you have the cash flow to pay it back immediately. (However, having lines of credit and overall business credit isn't such a bad idea. I know I didn't go into this much but once you have built a business and have positive cash flow consider getting a line of credit based on past performance to open the door for twice your liquid capital. This is what I've done and will continue to do as we grow. Feel free to hit me up on social media if you want more info on how I went about this for my business).

I believe if you take a loan, it's a sign of hard-headedness and I really hope you understand the decision you're making. If you pull it off, more power to you. But with entrepreneurship already being a risky path, I want you to be careful to consider all your options. Take your time and earn the money to start your business whether it's through self-funding, crowdfunding, grants, or pitch competitions. Embrace the grind and hustle it takes to earn money that way, and start your business off without digging yourself into a hole from day one.

LOOSE CHANGE

Pauleanna

The shoestring budget—I've been there and done that. I've been very transparent with you about how much debt I had in my early twenties, and I've never had rich parents, a baller boyfriend, or any financial investors drop cash to help me build my businesses. I funded every one of my businesses out of my pocket. Everything I purchased, flight I booked, freelancer I worked with, or service provider I hired got paid out of my paycheck. And sometimes, it was tight. Like, really tight.

But if I let having pennies in my bank account keep me from starting a business, I don't know if I'd be turning the kind of profit I am now. I had to step out on faith, stretch the hell out of my budget, and make it work. The good news is if I could make my pocket change work hard enough to get businesses off the ground, so can you. It's just going to take some discipline, hard work, and hustle to make money out of nothing.

Because cash isn't about to start falling out of the sky, here are some smart money tactics you can use to stretch a small budget far enough to build big businesses.

Hustle on the side.

In the same way that 9-to-5ers build businesses on the side or start side hustles to make extra cash, you may have to do some side hustling while you build your business to come up with the cash you need. One way to do this is to create additional products or services surrounding your main business. For example, if you're a blogger, you could offer blog post templates or content calendars to newbie bloggers who are just getting into the game. Or you could create a course or tutorial around your skillset and charge for access to your process. Both of those options are awesome because once you've created and marketed them, you can sit back and enjoy the passive income. If you have a little extra time, and people are interested in learning about what you do, you can tutor or coach people one-on-one (as long as you actually have the skills. Don't go charging people if you're expertise is weak).

Even if you can't figure out ways to create new services within your brand, you could do some good old-fashioned side hustling. Babysit for your friends and family members or purge your closet and sell the stuff you don't wear on eBay. Whatever it takes, just use what you have to make that extra cash.

Listen, don't be embarrassed or ashamed of what you need to do to make your dreams happen. I have a mentee in the beauty market starting a business of her own, but she moonlights as a bartender to make the cash to build her business. She was worried about whether people would question if she was truly an entrepreneur if they knew she had another job to keep the bills paid. But if she quit just to meet other people's expectations, her business would probably crumble without the money she pulls in. Don't let pride or perception keep you from hustling for your goals.

Figure out where you can cut.

If you can't make more, spend less. I'm willing to bet that somewhere in your budget, you're spending money on luxuries that you could really do without. I'm not saying to sacrifice your mani-pedi or morning coffee forever, but a few months without those extra perks put money in your pocket that could pay for something your business needs. Are you willing to be uncomfortable for a little bit, so you can build a business that's going to keep you paid for years?

If you're in a pinch and you literally can't find anywhere to cut frivolous spending (and I'm side-eyeing you here, because I think you might not be looking hard enough), you might have to consider skipping a bill to redirect the money. Now, chill, I'm not telling you to skip your bills on the regular. Don't screw up your credit. But sometimes, it needs to be done. When I first started getting serious about networking for business, I knew I needed to travel from Canada to the US. But I'd be looking at the ticket prices and then at my bank account, and thinking, "Bruh, I can't pay my bills and book this flight too." So, I'd weigh my options, and sometimes, the flight won out over phone bills and credit card payments because I knew the connection I'd make on that trip would pay off in the long run. It was a calculated risk, and not one I encourage you to make a habit out of, but there are times when that's the right move.

Know if DIYs are going to cost more in the long run.

There's some stuff you can do on your own in your business, but some things, you gotta spring for. I can't give you a definitive list of things you should or shouldn't DIY because that will depend on your skills. If a task falls in your wheelhouse, of course, you could do it yourself. If you're artsy and have some technical skills, you could create your own graphics. If you're a web designer, you can build your own website. When I started my website years ago, I wrote all the copy myself because I'm a writer. Duh. But I didn't build the site myself because I would have had no clue where to start and a sloppy website was not going to cut it. I paid for photography because image is an important part of your brand.

I'm not going to pretend this can't get expensive sometimes. Hiring an expert—a real expert—can be expensive, but it's worth it to get the best for your brand. I'll give you another example. The logo for my personal brand cost me $700. I definitely could have cheaped out and gone to Fiverr or worked with an amateur to cut the price down, but I play a long game. A logo is the face of your business. You can't play around with that. So I forked up the cash. For $700, I got a logo that I still love to this day. And it was a one and done thing. The designer got my vision right the very first time. The accuracy was incredible. To me, $700 was worth it because I got exactly what I wanted and needed and I've never had to look back.

I'm not advising you to spend beyond your means. You gotta know your budget and how much you can afford to push it. But always play to your strengths. When you're faced with costs, and you're considering a DIY, make sure you think about whether you really have the skills to pull it off, if you can afford the time to do it yourself, and if your customers or clients will be unimpressed if this thing isn't top quality. If the answer to either of those is no, scrounge up the cash and get a pro.

Work with interns.

Never, ever underestimate the value of working with interns. Before you spend cash on hiring staff you can't afford, ask around or get referrals for young people who have the skills you want and are willing to work for experience. If you're not sure where to look for interns, check out your local colleges. Students work hard, bruh. I know because a few colleges used to have me and my business on the list for students seeking internships. I used to get calls every semester with inquiries. I was confident in those interns because I knew they saw the internship as an investment in their education. I've had interns on my team handling things like social media, and it was a great experience. They gave me their best work, and with some direction, they were able to pull off exactly what I needed from them. In exchange, I took great care of them, gave them access to my services, products, and mentorship, and when it was time for them to move on, gave them great referrals that landed them paying positions.

Remember that money isn't the only currency.

If you don't have cash, find out what else you have that people value. I'm a writer, mentor, and speaker. Those are skills that people pay me for. That makes them currency too. Which means I can trade them or barter them. Say I wanted to work with a photographer who wanted a ghostwriter, we could work out an arrangement and figure out how many hours of photography would be of equal value to the piece they want written. It's a mutually beneficial situation where everybody gets what they want even if nó money is exchanged. As long as all parties are clear on the expectations from the get-go (contracts people!), this is a great system.

Cash in on your relationship capital.

If you've been building solid relationships with influential people, you have what's called relationship capital, and sometimes, that's worth way more than money. Because of relationships I created with dope entrepreneurs and business owners where I gave of my time, offered them help when they needed it, and was there when they needed me, I was able to confidently ask for their help when I needed access to spaces or resources I couldn't pay my way into. For example, I've been featured as an expert on TV because I befriended producers and casting directors. I've been featured in Essence Magazine because I'm tight with one of the writers who thinks of me when my brand aligns with her articles. My friend who's an executive at LinkedIn is pitching me to her team for a video series. And I have a friend who's a strategist for Nike, and when they were looking for inspiring career women for a campaign, he reached out to me. I'm not even kidding. These are everyday conversations for me because I've got friends who can help me make moves. What's your circle looking like? I'm not telling you to start relationships simply for what you can get out of them. But there's nothing wrong with tapping your network when you need to if you've put in the work to deserve to.

You also want to get in good with the media. When it's time to promote your latest venture or get some publicity, having good relationships with journalists and editors can help you get your name in print or land you a dope interview absolutely free. Sometimes making those contacts is as simple as searching the contact page on your ideal media outlets' websites, or hitting up Twitter or LinkedIn and doing a keyword search for "editor" + the publication you're looking for. Then follow them and interact organically. Please do not be that person that slides into someone's DMs and you've literally never spoken to them before. That's asking for a block and delete, and there's no coming back from that. Keep it natural, be genuine, and when the time comes to make an ask, you just might get a yes.

I know, probably better than a lot of people, that the financial part of business is hard, and even harder when your pockets are empty, and your bank account is in the negative. But I also know that you can make things happen when you really want to. Stretch yourself, stretch your budget, and make your business happen.

MORE MONEY, MORE POWER

Pauleanna

Alright, we've talked about finding money for funding and stretching what you have to cover your costs, but we need to tackle how you're going to make sure that your businesses are turning a profit. I started my first business in 2007 in the fashion industry. While I made money, it wasn't enough to live on. It wasn't until 2016 that I made a real profit and could cut myself a salary of $40,000. 2017 was one my most profitable years with my businesses yet. For the first time, I hit six figures ($110,721 to be exact). I'm still a little shocked when I think about how much I was able to make with businesses that I operate while I still spend at least eight hours a day at a corporate job. The goal has always been to put myself in a position where I could pay my mom's bills so she can chill. In fact, I just sent her a money transfer for $1,000, just because. In my prayers, I always ask God to bless me so I can bless others. It feels really good to see the hard work pay off in such a significant way. And those profits are allowing me to set up even bigger moves for the years to come as I now have the funds to invest in the things that build my business, like staff and travel.

I'm not going to lie to you, a lot of the financial success I've had recently has come because I stopped making some of the money mistakes that were killing my profits, and started putting processes and actions in place to keep the cash flowing in. In 2017, my income exclusively from my businesses jumped significantly into the 6-figure territory. I started my personal brand in 2009, didn't start making any real money until 2015 and then finally found my rhythm last year. If that's not patience, I don't know what is. That's not a brag; use it as motivation. If you're struggling with getting your profits where you want them to be, I want to share some tips with you.

Find your 1,000 true fans.

The originator of this theory, Kevin Kelly, wrote an essay in 2008. Here's an excerpt:

"To be a successful creator you don't need millions. You don't need millions of dollars, millions of customers, millions of clients, or millions of fans. To make a living as a craftsperson, photographer, musician, designer, author, animator, app maker, entrepreneur, or inventor you need only thousands of true fans.

A true fan is defined as a fan that will buy anything you produce. These diehard fans will drive 200 miles to see you sing; they will buy the hardback and paperback and audible versions of your book, they will purchase your next figurine sight unseen; they will pay for the best-of DVD version of your free YouTube channel; they will come to your chef's table once a month. If you have roughly a thousand true fans like this (also known as super fans), you can make a living...if you are content to make a living but not a fortune." - Kevin Kelly

I started blogging in 2009 and public speaking in 2010. I've had supporters (I don't like the word "fans" too much) literally grow with me ever since. For this, I've gone out of my way to show my appreciation. It's a two-way street. These close-knit relationships I've built with my audience have been the biggest driver for many paid referrals, sold out events, award nominations and even an endorsement of my book from Queen Latifah herself.

Jab, Jab, Jab, Right Hook.

This is how I got my supporters to ride with me through it all. Long before Gary Vaynerchuk developed this now-popular phrase, I was practicing this business strategy. If you don't have a clue what I'm talking about, Google it. Both Gary, and his book. Here's the gist of it: "Your story needs to move people's spirits and build their goodwill so that when you finally do ask them to buy from you, they feel like you've given them so much it would almost be rude to refuse."

(Some) new business owners or side hustlers I've met have yet to understand the concept of giving shit away for free and expecting nothing in return. Generosity is the very best business strategy. I've used it since day one and have never had an empty sales funnel since. Whether through my newsletter, blog content, vlog series, podcast, social media, thank you notes, conference calls, meet & greets, book giveaways, and more—it all matters. The consumer needs to build an emotional connection through your work. People want to see the real you. Don't play pretend so that you can look more attractive. Choose purpose over popularity. Like my mentor always says, you should tell the story behind the glory. It's about emotionally connecting with your audience and communicating your story so that it is clear, consistent and compelling. Stop pushing the service or product and start pushing your story. Those who do the work, win. Those who don't, don't. Build your brand by telling the truth.

Master your sales pitch (or hire someone who is brilliant at it).

Every business owner needs to know how to sell. It is essential. I know you don't want to, but without truly understanding how to sell yourself (organically), you've already lost. No pressure. A great resource that has helped me is Nisha Moodley's Free to Say Yes. It's an eBook and voice note. She explains, in full detail, a 7-step sales process that gives clients the freedom to say yes. When I first started out in business, I used her formula, and it is amazing. At this point, I'm extremely comfortable. I could sell you a napkin and make you believe it will change your entire life.

But above all else, know your shit. If you have a product or service to sell, you need to know everything and anything about it. Study your industry inside out and be ready for any follow up questions (because someone like me will ask them before I decide to buy). A key lesson I learned is people don't buy services/products, they buy the transformation they expect as a result of using your service/product. So focus more on the experience you can provide rather than your title. At the very least you should have your personal brand statement down. This 30-second elevator pitch could make or break you.

Don't sell your time, sell your impact.

As a speaker, I often go into organizations and talk about things like social media and branding that help those organizations turn a profit. Sometimes, I'm looking out at an audience of 150 people who are all going to go away with the knowledge I just dropped and use it to make themselves and their company more money. Sure, I could charge the organization for the 30-60 minutes that I spent on their stage. But the value they got wasn't just how long I was standing up there, but how impactful what I said is going to be on their bottom line. So, I charge accordingly. It was a tip my speaking mentor gave me. When I decide on the rate for speeches, I charge based on how many people I'm going to be speaking to, how much I think the information is worth, the level of preparation I need to do and any travel costs I need to cover.

If you've got a service-based business, I'd suggest you come up with a similar payment model. If you're a web designer, charge according to how much business a killer website is going to pull in for a company. Logo designer? How much of an impact is a high-quality luxury logo going to have on your customer's client base? Even if you choose to use an hourly rate, make sure you base that rate on how much value your services are bringing to your client and not just on how many hours you spend working with them. When you charge according to impact instead of time, your profits are no longer crunched by how many hours are in a day.

Stop charging peanuts and raise your prices.

Now, I'm not telling you to raise your prices through the roof, especially if your level of expertise and skill don't warrant you charging people a whole check. But if you're good at what you do, and you have receipts to prove it, you absolutely should raise your prices. For two reasons: 1) you deserve to earn your worth, and 2) you'll start attracting high-end clients who can pay you the kind of money you'd like to make. If your prices are too low, you'll only ever make too little.

Freelance expert Shanita Hubbard dropped some knowledge on her Twitter about the importance of not undercharging. "When you lowball yourself it is harmful. You get locked into that rate. Folks talk...If you are asked about your [rates], and you're afraid of lowballing yourself, you should reply with something like, 'My rates vary depending on different factors. What is your budget?'" Her advice is solid, and I encourage you to follow it, so you don't get stuck making less than you deserve.

Stretch yourself and your clients with your rates.

I recently had a realtor approach me about penning a project for her, and I was originally going to quote her $5,000. I had it written down and everything. And then right at the moment when she asked me how much, "$10,000" came out of my mouth instead. I almost couldn't believe myself. But she agreed. Had I gone with my original quote, I would have undercharged and left $5,000 on the table. I had another ghostwriting client warn me that he had a small budget and asked me to be fair. I honestly had no idea what a small budget meant. He wasn't specific, and that threw me for a loop because I really didn't know what I could reasonably ask for. I eventually came up with a quote somewhere in the $12,000 range. For me, it was stretching myself, but in the end, he agreed to the price. The thing is, both clients hesitated a little, and that's understandable. I'm not asking for pocket change. But in the end, they both were on board.

I tell you this story to highlight the two ways to know if you're not charging enough. First off, if when you quote potential clients, you don't feel even a little bit nervous, you're not charging enough. No one likes to feel like they're asking too much, so a lot of the times, entrepreneurs set their rates too low so as not to scare clients off or seem too bold. But be bold, even if it scares you. And secondly, if you never have a single client hesitate before agreeing to your rates, you're likely undercharging. I'm not telling you to crush anybody's budget, but your services should feel like an investment. If your price is always easily accepted, I guarantee you're leaving money on the table and underestimating your value to your customers.

Learn to stop giving your money away.

You'd be amazed by how much money you're losing by giving away time and energy that you should be charging for. If you're not charging for consultations or turning down people who want to ask you a million questions that will basically help them create their own business, you're missing key opportunities for profit. Don't get me wrong, there's nothing wrong with being helpful and answering a question or two, but your expertise is valuable, and you can't just be giving it away to anyone who slides into your DMs to quiz you.

You spent time, energy, and money acquiring the knowledge that you have, which means you absolutely can put a dollar value on it. Marie Forleo has a quote about this that I absolutely love. She says, "If they want to pick your brain, ask them to pick a time and a method of payment. Because if you want people to value your time, you need to put a value on it." Perfect advice. Don't forget that all the time you spend answering DMs and sitting down in coffee shops giving people free advice is time you're not spending working on things that put cash in your pocket.

If you find you're fielding lots of requests from people to pick your brain, here are a few things you can do to get them out of your inbox and onto your client list:

Politely let them know you charge for consultations and direct them to your booking calendar. (If you don't have one, get Calendly).

If they want the info bad enough, they'll book and pay up. If they were just looking for a free ride, they'll be out of your hair. It's a win either way.

Direct them to free resources.

If you've got free resources that might answer their questions, let them know to check those out. That might help to convert them into paying clients too. If you don't have anything that might answer their questions for free, you can tip them off to a free resource you know that might help.

Find out what they want before you agree to coffee.

The coffee date thing is exactly how people rope you in. If you're cool with a coffee date where you dish industry info, that's fine. But if you're adamant about not doing consultations for free, make sure that when that friend, acquaintance, or family member invites you to coffee, that you both know up front you're only down if you're not talking business.

Spend time with people who have the kind of bank account you want.

If you want to be successful, you need to rub shoulders (and or study) the habits of successful people. Their energy will rub off on you. If you cannot connect with anyone personally, there's always the Internet. I study one Fortune 500 CEO monthly. I'll read every article, watch every talk, follow them closely on social media — I don't miss a beat. Another random habit I have is to drive around wealthy neighborhoods. I'm such a believer in the law of attraction. I will literally sit on the side of the road and envision my plot of land right where I am. I did it when I was dead ass broke and still do it now that I'm in a better position financially. No dream is too big.

At the end of the day, how much you make is up to you. If you've got a good product or service, it's how you price yourself that determines how much of a profit you're going to turn. Implementing these tips (along with some of the other money advice I've offered in earlier chapters like investing and diversifying your income) won't necessarily increase your earnings right away, but in the long run, these smart money moves will help you build your bottom line.

THE REAL DEAL ON CHARITY

Andrew

Our goal throughout this book is to help you find success, and I'm not going to pretend that has nothing to do with making money. Your business can't be considered truly successful if you never turn a profit. Revenue is a key part of the game whether you're selling t-shirts or providing business consultation. But I do think that now and then, businesses should make some time to focus on giving back.

If you pay attention to businesses and branding, you'd realize that almost every major successful business has charitable foundations or affiliations. McDonald's has the Ronald McDonald House which helps sick children and their families. Walmart works with Feeding America to provide fruits and vegetables to people in need. And Google donates to a bunch of charities, including a non-profit that gives cash donations to the poor and a school for blind children. Giving back is a part of the ethos of a lot of major brands. So, should it be part of yours? Honestly, only if you genuinely feel that it should.

Don't give for show. Your customers will side-eye you.

Giving back is an amazing thing to do, but it shouldn't be just something you do for the 'gram. There's marketing charity that's all about making your brand look generous, and then there's the real deal – genuine charity that's all about helping people. Giving back shouldn't solely be a business decision. You can't look at social entrepreneurship as something to do just because others are doing it. Long term, if that's not what you or your business really stand for, people will feel it's not real, and it will turn them off. Make sure that your intentions are in the right place before you give a dime.

If you're not sure if you're giving for the right reasons, ask yourself if you would still make the donation if you couldn't tell anyone about it. If the answer is no, then you're doing it to impress people, and that can't be your motive. It's always funny to me when someone posts a picture or video of themselves on social media claiming they're amazing because they give to people on the streets. Like, who does that? What are their real intentions? I highly suggest you watch Poverty Inc. a documentary on Netflix that will explain the good intentions of charity but also the negative effects it has beyond the initial layer of the good deed. To keep it simple, if you're giving and you have to create a press release, it's obvious that you're not really interested in helping others.

If you're going to give, pick wisely.

I do think that businesses that have charities that are publicized are dope. And I'm sure many of them do it out of a genuine interest in helping the people and organizations they donate to. But as much as giving back shouldn't strictly be a business decision, you do have to consider how the causes you choose reflect your brand and impact your customers. Because social entrepreneurship done right does make people feel good about your brand. They feel great about supporting a business that's connected to causes that matter to them. Which means you should be donating to causes that fit with your brand and the values you share with your customer base.

I do have a caution for brands that are just getting up off the ground. If money's tight, cash donations probably aren't your best bet.

You can't give what you don't got.

We can't all be Bill Gates. He gives away millions, and he can do that because he has billions. Even if your intentions are good, giving before you've secured the bag for yourself is a bad move. If you're not able to give financially, you're hurting yourself more than you're helping the world. So many young people want to give and do charity work, which is great, but they're not understanding that if you give when your cup is empty, you're giving inches away. Rather than taking two steps back to take ten steps forward in impact, you're moving inches at a time because you're giving more than you can afford. I always tell people, do what you want to do, but don't complain when you don't get the results you want because you weren't strategic and disciplined. Yes, this even applies to charity. If your good deeds are killing your business, that's an L. You need to be in a position of abundance where you can give freely without jeopardizing your success. You have to give according to what you can spare. If your budget is stretched all the way out to cover operation costs and just keep the door open, you can't afford to be giving away cash. But like we said earlier in this chapter, money isn't the only currency.

When money is low, give the most valuable asset in the world – time.

If you really want to give, go volunteer at a shelter or with a local community cause. Change someone's life with your time. Somewhere in between your grind, you can spare a couple of hours to volunteer. You can even integrate it into your business. Take your staff and volunteer at a soup kitchen or whatever cause aligns with your company's values.

Whether you choose to give back on the low or make your charitable work and donations a public part of your brand, just make sure you're doing it from a good place. Always do what feels genuine and true to your business, whether it's public or not, because branding is a matter of the heart.

Pauleanna

I absolutely believe that businesses should be giving back. The whole reason we're able to make a profit at all is because the community supports us by buying our products and services. I think that once we get into a position to give back, however much or little, we should. And like Andrew says, we should do it for the cause, not the applause. Giving back isn't about validation or praise but to genuinely benefit the people that we help. And when you're able to have that real and genuine impact, you make sure that your business has long-term value in the community too.

Truly solve an issue, and you'll always have a place in the hearts of your community.

Businesses that have a positive impact on the communities they serve are more likely to experience longevity because they solve issues that matter in those spaces. A perfect example is jewelry brand, Rebel Nell. Based in Detroit, the brand sells beautiful pieces of jewelry designed from bits and pieces of graffiti found around the city. But there's another layer to Rebel Nell that makes them a community highlight. The brand employs disadvantaged women from Detroit to make the jewelry. While they create these beautiful designs, Rebel Nell also provides them with information on wellness, business, and financial management to help them transition into owning businesses of their own. This is a brand that's going to last because they're not just selling a product and making a profit, but they're also solving a problem for women in the community who benefit from the employment and skills development Rebel Nell offers.

Another great company that is nailing this is TOMS. It's impressive how hard they work to address social issues, locally and around the world. Their 2017 impact reports state that customer purchases for the year provided "9.4 million new pairs of shoes, 102,000 people with restored sight, 103,000 weeks of safe water, 41,000 safe births, 15,000 bullying prevention and support services, and 20,000 people with a year of solar light." That's incredible. But giving back is a huge part of their company ethos, and they give their customers the opportunity to be an active part of that work as well by donating a portion of every purchase to these causes.

Even if your brand doesn't have social impact so directly interwoven into your mission or daily operation, it's important that you find a way to serve the community and spaces you operate in. Even if your business is primarily online, there are ways you can connect to people and causes in your online community who have a problem that your service or product can help with.

Play your charitable role.

It can be overwhelming when you hear stories like TOMS' because you may not be able to give nearly that much yet. But that's fine. This is one of those things where you stay in your lane and give in the way that best suits your business. I started a small scholarship through my mentorship program New Girl on the Block that's open to girls and young women who need help paying for school. It's not enough to cover a full year's tuition, but I made it as much as I can afford, and for a young woman who's trying to create the future she wants, it's something that gets her a step closer.

You may only be able to help one person a year with an offer of pro bono services, or you may have to lead a fundraiser or donation drive and encourage the community to get involved rather than coming up with the donations on your own. As long as you do what you can, that's still something, and the impact is still real.

Give back within your own space.

While you're thinking of ways to give back to the community, don't forget that sometimes the community is closer than you think. I've worked with over 150 women through New Girl on the Block as I helped to mentor them through their career and entrepreneurial goals. Their mentorship fee covers customized advice and mentorship calls for life planning, career development, and personal branding. But when my girls need me, I'm there way beyond the terms of the contract we've signed. I've helped mentees escape prostitution and stripping. I've shown up when I received teary calls from suicidal mentees. I booked flights to Philly and New York for girls who'd never been outside of Toronto so they could be exposed to new possibilities. I do all of it because I realize that as much as these young ladies are clients, they are a part of my community too, and I go above and beyond for them because that's what my brand is all about.

I want to encourage you to look to brands like TOMS and Rebel Nell as an example, but recognize that it's a lofty one. Your business is new, and you're still building your brand. But there's a lot to be learned from brands that make social entrepreneurship a priority. Study up on them, learn what you can, and scale their practices to fit and suit your brand.

Chapter 14:
Make Them Want You

SUPPLY WHAT'S MISSING

Andrew

There are probably hundreds of people in your industry with similar skills, expertise, and ideas as you. So how do create your own lane and stand out from the competition? Slow down. I know it might seem counterintuitive because you want to launch now and get your business going and growing. But rushing isn't the way to make that happen. Quick quote from the Canadian Prince himself, Drake: "It's not about who did it first. It's about who did it best." Rushing to get your idea out is not going to guarantee you success. Making it in business, especially if you're in a market with a lot of competition, is a long game, and it takes time.

I know that to a lot of people, it looked like I left my 9-to-5 and became a full-time entrepreneur overnight, but getting there was two years in the making before I left my job! My idea for The O Agency started a year before anyone even knew what it was. I spent that time evaluating, challenging, researching, and testing out my ideas. I was thinking about how to make the O Agency amazing every minute of the day—in the shower, at work, during dinner, in my sleep. I spent a lot of time looking at what would work and chipping away at the things that wouldn't. I had to work out all the details with clients, strategy, website. Even when I had the business end ready, the brand launch took over six months to plan to perfection. Those two years of prep have helped me create a business that is still booming today.

If you want a business that's going to fall on its face in six months and get drowned out by the competition, then go ahead and rush. All you'll have to show for it is a flash that fizzles out fast and is forgotten even faster. If you want to build something that's going to last, take your time and move with purpose and focus on the behind-the-scenes work that makes for real impact.

If you know the service you want to offer—and by this point, you should be pretty clear on that—then the next thing you need to figure out is who you're trying to sell it to.

Serving everybody is for the birds. Nail down who your ideal customer is.

When I asked my friend Shawn Johnson what the biggest mistake he ever made in business was, he said trying to be too much for too many people because it brought down the quality of his service overall. It's a common mistake. A lot of early entrepreneurs get caught up in trying to sell to everybody. You ask them who their target market is, and they give you these vague generalizations like men and women between 18 and 65. That's highly ineffective. Do you know how many different kinds of people fit into those categories? That's like trying to sell the same product or service to a poor teenage kid and someone's rich grandma. Not an easy task, and there's no reason why they wouldn't both choose two separate companies that are doing the work to target them specifically.

When I say figure out who you're selling to, I encourage you to get really specific and develop a buyer persona. Your buyer persona needs to consider basics like age, location, gender, race, education and income levels. But then dive in even deeper into things like lifestyle, personality, attitude, opinions, interests, emotions, deepest fears, and biggest goals. If you know who exactly your customer is, it will be easy to speak to them directly in ways that other brands might not.

This is something I excel at because I have deep cultural perspective. Remember, I spent ten years in an Asian/immigrant household. Then, when I was twelve, I moved to PG County in Maryland and pretty much went to an all-black middle school, high school, and college. From the ages of 12-22, I was immersed in the experiences in the African American community, which is very different than just learning about people on TV. After Hampton, I spent six years in corporate America, startup villages, and co-working spaces that were predominantly White American. I got to understand the tiniest nuances of how they think and move. All of that experience has brought me to the conclusion that everybody thinks their feelings and thoughts and views are right because that's what they've lived. This understanding allows me to not worry about convincing anybody to change their mind. Rather, I just learn to speak their language and relate in a way that's advantageous to my goals, legacy, and the community I want to "put on."

Find out what pain your service will ease for them.

Once you've figured out who you're trying to sell to, you need to figure you why they'd buy your service. And I'm not talking about how cool your product is, or what your product does on paper. You need to know what life problem or desire you and your business can help them handle. Get to know their pain points, figure out how to soothe them, and you have a much better chance of locking them in.

Get eyes on the competition and scope out how they're winning.

No matter how much you narrow your target market, it's possible that other businesses in your industry are trying to reach them too. So, you need to know where they're at and what they're doing. Hit up Google and study your competitors who are really succeeding in the market. Check out their social media, websites, and content to see what kind of language, audience engagement, and marketing practices they're using. Industry conferences and related Facebook groups will also help you get some insight into what your competition is up to.

Once you know the standard, raise it.

Because you know what your competition is doing, you now know what your target market expects from a service like yours. If you want to carve out your own lane, you're going to have to do more than just meet that expectation. You need to raise the bar. If there are things your competitors are falling short on, step up and do better. Maybe that's offering amazing customer service, using your skills or forging partnerships to add extra value to your service offering, or making every customer feel like you custom-built your business for them. And never make customers have to struggle to work with you. Keep your website user-friendly, contact info easy to find, and communication on point.

Spot a gap and fill it.

Part of raising the standard is discovering the things that other businesses have completely failed to do for your target market and get them done. Best way to figure that out is to test your competitions' product and service (or speak to people who have) and find out what parts of it could be better. Pay attention to the complaints people have about businesses like yours and figure out how to resolve them. You may even want to find a better way to provide the services already being offered. Think Netflix; they took the Friday-night-movie-on-the-couch-experience and made it easier by cutting out the trip to the video store and making thousands of titles available for one monthly price. Same product—movies—but a totally different delivery style that made life easier for customers.

Test your ideas and be prepared to switch up.

While understanding your competition is important, studying and testing the ideas you come up with is even more key. Doing all the research in the world isn't going to tell you for sure if your product/service/business approach is going to be successful. And unless your family and friends are your target market, their feedback isn't going to cut it either. The only people who can confirm that for you is your target market. So, test out your ideas on them. If you've built an email list or social media following of members of your target audience, survey them and get their feedback on your ideas. Create a beta test product or service and offer it at a discounted rate in exchange for honest commentary. Or, if you can afford to, offer the service for free to a small test group who really fit your market to see how they feel about it.

Then use what they say to determine if you're on track. Be prepared that you might have spent months working on something, and your test group might spot a fault you somehow missed completely. If that's the case, don't be stubborn. Humble out, go back to the drawing board, ditch the things that don't work at all, tweak the things that need adjusting, and try again.

None of this work is glamorous. It's not exciting. It's not good material for flexin' on the 'gram or bragging to your friends. It's the tedious stuff that requires spending hours and hours of research and learning and studying. But it's this stuff that builds the foundation for the big launch, the huge profits, and the Instagram-worthy stories. Remember, it's the work that nobody sees that builds empires.

MARKETING 101

Pauleanna

No matter how dope your brand is, if you don't market it, it's going to stay a dope secret. Yeah, enigma has its perks, but it's a difficult marketing tactic to pull off, and for brands and businesses that are just starting out, it's a dangerous game to play. It's important that as you build your business, you develop an effective marketing strategy that will help you get the right eyes on your business.

Marketing is what allows you to build your tribe—the people who are loyal to you and your brand and will support you as you grow your brand. That's why massive brands spend millions of dollars every year on advertising, social media and brand partnership. Although you may not have that kind of budget, it's still essential that you create and execute an effective marketing strategy to put the spotlight on your brand. Here are a few cost-effective tactics I've used over the years:

Let your clients sell your business for you.

Feedback from clients goes a very long way. Not only does it help you understand what the consumer likes about your product or service, but it's also an endorsement that can help persuade potential clients of how dope you are. In the same way that Yelp reviews can help you decide if you want to try out a new restaurant, client testimonials can help potential customers who are on the fence decide if you're worth the investment.

People love free ish, so let them have it.

In Chapter 13, we talked about not giving away too much for free, but there are times when it's a good move. You just have to be smart about it.

Generosity really is one of the cornerstones of my brand. I give, give and give some more. Because who doesn't like getting things for free. A great time to do this is during a pre-launch. For example, before the release of my novel Everything I Couldn't Tell My Mother, I gave my audience a free 4-chapter download just to tease them a little. It was a win on so many fronts. My mailing list opt-ins blew up, awareness of my book and brand spread significantly, and people were eager to have the finished book when I launched it. Pre-orders for the book were sold out for three weeks before the launch. Seducing my readers with a free sample was a power move that helped me turn a profit when the time was right.

And that's just one of many examples. On the day of the book launch, I gave free copies to the 200 people who showed up. I gave free copies to over 250 people who showed up. As a result, one of my biggest press opportunities happened. Remember my mention about Queen Latifah? Well this is where it all started. I created an experience so good, my consumers never forgot. In fact, a few short months later, when the Queen Latifah show did a call out on Twitter asking its following what they were reading that summer, my squad raised their hands and vouched for me. Next thing I knew my novel was showcased on the Queen Latifah Show website as a top summer read. That shit went viral - the love for my book, of course. So many people stood up for me and it was because I spent years giving quality to them. If you're looking for ideas of things you can create and give away for free, consider:

1.   E-books
2.   Worksheets
3.   Informative conference calls
4.   Meet and greets
5.   Live workshops
6.   Consultations
7.   Newsletters

These are just a few ideas on a basic level. Figure out what makes sense to your brand and what your audience would like and roll with it.

Turn friends into influencers with an affiliate program.

Have people who were already interested in your product and service do some promotion in exchange for a commission on referrals that result in a sale. It's a smart move that uses their excitement for your brand to get access to their audience.

Call in a favor.

If you've been networking your ass off and you've made some friends in high places, or if you have a friend who knows somebody who could be helpful, you've got an in. Be prepared to take it when you get a chance to strut your stuff. For example, my mentor Shannon Boodram helped me get on MTV, my friend Sheldon Neil got me on Global Television, and my friend Annalie got me on CBC, and so on. The stories are endless. I've given several other examples throughout this book of how friends, mentors, and connections have helped me get opportunities I wanted. Trust me, favors come in handy when you have a business. Just remember that, when the time comes, you should be prepared to pay it forward. Friendships should always be mutually beneficial. Always. There's nothing wrong with calling in a favor, but nobody likes a leech. If you always take more than you give, your friendships are going to die. Just as much as you want to be able to call on people in your life, you should be ready to think of them when chances come up to help them get opportunities they deserve.

Go a step beyond pics and create a dope video.

You can throw hundreds of words at your audience and give them bomb ass photos every day, but video takes things to a whole other level. If you develop a creative visual that is educational, emotional, and entertaining, that's the kind of thing that goes viral. Your audience will love it, and they'll be hype to share it with others over social media. Again, free promo.

Get some face time with your market by hosting an event in your city.

Whether it's a pre-launch, a launch, a thank you party, film screening, workshop, meet and greet, or vision board party, I've embraced the opportunities I've had to meet up with clients and other people I could work with. It's a smart move because it not only promotes you and your brand, but it gives you a chance to talk to the people you're marketing to, hear their feedback and concerns, and answer their questions. The emotional connection this lets you forge builds loyalty, which is one of the most priceless assets a business can have.

Leave sloppy, basic websites in 1999.

Seriously, your website is one of your biggest marketing tools. Marie Forleo just cut right to the chase when she said, "You need a website that sells and doesn't suck." You seriously do. It is worth the investment to upgrade your website so you can attract more traffic. If your website is looking lackluster right now, make moves to upgrade it. Whether you need to change your brand colors to be more in line with your brand vision, create better quality content on your blog, renovate your online store, add dope video content, or start from scratch, spend the time and money to get it done. Not sure what works well? Look at the personalities, bloggers, and brands you admire and take notes. Ask yourself what makes you keep going back for more? What do you love about their site? If you're still lost, get a branding expert or a website developer to help you work it out.

The key to good marketing is to make sure that everything you put in front of your customers is truly representative of your brand and that it's something your target audience is going to love. But don't overthink it. Everything I just suggested can be summed up in five simple steps:

1. Start with what you know (Share your expertise)
2. Add a personal touch (Be yourself)
3. Be remarkable (Blow your audience away)
4. Practice generosity (Give your tribe what they want)
5. Be consistent (Stay in your lane).

If you make all your marketing moves with these things in mind, you'll be golden.

CUT THE COMMERCIALS

Pauleanna

I'm a networking maven. I use social media to build powerful relationships and push my brand. I love sharing magical moments just like anyone else, but let's make something very clear. Accumulating likes, comments and followers should never be your main focus. Having a positive online presence is a good look, but fishing for attention is lame and not necessary. And it's no way to create a brand that people are going to be on board with. Cut the commercials.

It's so important that if you're using social media as a marketing tool that you don't let curation turn into faking it. You absolutely should be selective about what you post, and make sure that everything you share online is in line with the brand image you've developed, but it shouldn't come off as ingenuine. As both Andrew and I have said more than a few times, people can smell a fake from a thousand miles away.

It's like those infomercials that come on late at night for things like ShamWow or Slap Chop. Remember those ads? Dramatic, over-the-top and just mad salesy. Those commercials might be a bit persuasive at 3 in the morning when you're sleepy, but realistically, you know they're ridiculous. The same rules apply to your social media. If it comes off like everything you post is part of one big long advertisement, people are going to check out fast. What you need to do instead is put authenticity at the forefront and let your audience really get to know your brand.

Start by getting real, even if real is ugly.

As a mentor and motivational speaker, storytelling is a huge part of my brand. But I don't just tell the stories about my wins and successes. I talk about my past, share my struggles, and reveal my imperfections. I let people know that I'm not flawless and I didn't get where I am without some bumps in the road.

An amazing example I saw of this recently was Demetria Lucas, the relationship expert who has authored two books about love and dating and answered over 60,000 questions in her online advice column. After her marriage ended in divorce, she posted on her Instagram about the experience and got really vulnerable with her followers. It was amazing to see because her transparency was met by a lot of positive support from her audience. To some, a divorce might have seemed like a shot to her credibility, but by leveling with her audience instead of hiding her ugly truth, she reassured them that they could trust her to be real.

For personal brands, this is important. It takes some courage, but it allows your audience to connect with you as a human being. But even for other kinds of businesses, it's possible to let audiences see the real too. Whether that's sharing about the process it took to get to a final product or giving people a glimpse behind-the-scenes at the office, give your followers a chance to see more than perfection.

Put your personality into everything.

The key to keeping it real isn't the sappy stories. It's the transparency. Don't be afraid to do that no matter what comments might come your way or what people might think. Transparency has a ripple effect. You build loyalty and engagement, and it makes brands want to work with you. Perfect example — Karen Civil. She was approached by Beats by Dre in their early years because they liked the way she had branded herself online. They asked her to help them discover their online voice and develop their digital marketing. She nailed being herself, and because of that, other brands trusted her to help them figure out how to be authentic too.

Divert from your content calendar now and then.

Content calendars are great to make sure your content is on point, and you don't leave your audience hanging. But some of the best social media moments aren't planned. Great posts come out of the thoughts that hit you on a whim or genuine responses to current events or day-to-day occurrences. Embrace those.

Show off your work-in-progress.

If you've got a cool project in the works, let people know how it's coming along. I love when visual artists post videos or snapshots of the pieces they're working on. It builds up excitement to see the finished thing, but it also lets people get a peep at the kind of work, time, and effort it takes to pull off the final product.

Give up some of the insider goods.

If you stumble across cool resources or have tips that you think would be helpful to your customer base, don't be afraid to share it with them. And if your friends are doing dope things, share that too. Yes, you establish your brand online to attract customers, but it shouldn't be all about you.

If you're still struggling to figure out how to make your social media presence feel professional but authentic, check out some of my faves like Alex Elle, Alex Wolf, Hayet Rida, Dana Chanel and Dana Falsetti, just to name a few. These are people that have really nailed the honesty and transparency it takes to build trust with an audience. The great thing is, not all of their social posts and stories are about tear-jerking moments. They share the highlights too. But everything feels genuine.

Andrew

If you want to become a blogger, entrepreneur, digital marketer, or social influencer, say this with me right now: "I don't care about getting more followers. Let me change the lives of the people following me right now." If that made you uncomfortable, you need to shift your mentality. If you noticed, nothing about Pauleanna's advice for building an authentic social media presence had anything to do with follower counts and other shallow metrics. Way too many people believe that big social media followings are the defining factor of success, and that's a huge lie. As someone people often turn to for help to build their brands, I've worked with people in the 100,000 to one million followers range, but their brands don't have much to show for it. Don't let the follow count fool you.

Building brand awareness should be about way more than just putting on a front for the sake of looking influential. It needs to be about having real influence on real people. One of my personal brand goals in 2017 was to go deeper. Beyond the surface level things like followers, views, likes, and shallow interactions. One of the most effective ways I found to make this happen is to get offline.

Don't let social media be the only way you build your brand.

Follow Pauleanna's advice and create a social media presence that genuinely reflects your brand, but please don't let it stop there. Social media shouldn't be the entirety of your brand identity because it can't build a brand, it can only optimize it. Whenever you get opportunities to connect with people about your brand in person, take them. Face-to-face interactions let you show enthusiasm, personality, and expertise in ways that a picture and a caption just can't.

Get into spaces where you can access your audience offline.

Find out where the relevant industry conferences, trade shows, and events are being hosted. These are the perfect opportunities to start developing an offline following. Whether you choose to get a vendor table, take speaking opportunities, or just show up at the event as a regular attendee with your business cards in hand, don't miss out on these chances to build solid connections with people and give them a chance to see that what you present online matches what you and your brand does offline too.

Oh yeah, business cards still matter.

In a world that's moving digital so fast, a lot of people feel like business cards don't matter. But this is one of those old-fashioned marketing tactics that still works. Imagine you're at an event talking to someone who's loving everything you say about your business and you can tell they're down to work with you. Then they ask you for a card so they can hit you up later, and you have to tell them you don't have one. C'mon man. Saying you don't have a card can leave people questioning whether you're serious. Get cards. A clean, simple on-brand design with all the relevant info anyone would need to get in touch with you later is a good bet for anybody.

Give people way more than business cards with experiential marketing.

You don't have to wait for someone else to host an event or for strangers to ask you for business cards to get your offline marketing game on. In a nutshell, experiential marketing is a live, interactive brand experience. Dope example: Adidas created a pop-up shop called the "D Rose Jump Store" where NBA players challenged fans to jump 10 feet for a chance to grab a pair of sneakers for free. You know everybody who was there is probably going to remember that event forever. I'm not saying you have to book an NBA player, but with a little bit of creativity (and maybe a bit of cash), you can create an offline marketing experience that will give you a chance to showcase your brand in a way people won't forget.

These offline marketing techniques give you a chance to do something that's just not possible online—you give people the real deal, completely unfiltered. Whether it's something as simple as chatting with a potential client for five minutes or as high-level as an event that gives people a taste of how cool your brand is, don't miss opportunities to build your brand in the real world and show people that you're just as dope offline as you are on the 'gram.

Chapter 15:
Friends in High Places

<hr>

THE ICEBREAKER

<hr>

Pauleanna

Have you ever heard the saying, "Your network is your net worth"? In entrepreneurship, this isn't a cool IG caption, it's a fact. When you're starting a business and creating a brand, it's essential that you don't try to do it in isolation. Building a network and developing solid relationships is a must. It's networking that lets you make the connections that allow you to build things like relationship capital, find your tribe and reach out to your target market, meet dope people for collaborations and partnerships, meet potential brand ambassadors, and gain access to your dream clients. If you create a solid brand and have killer marketing, you'll attract people to you, but establishing a strong network isn't something that happens to you. It's something you have to actively work on.

Networking is not something I play about. I'm constantly working on meeting brilliant people in my industry, planning pitches to my dream clients, and forging connections who can help me get access to the people and spaces I want to be in. Remember my story about my flight to New

York that left me sleeping on the floor of the airport? All for the sake of meeting with someone who eventually helped me land a position as a Forbes contributor. I told you, I don't play when it comes to networking. It's always high on my to-do list.

If you've been slacking on networking because you're not totally comfortable with the idea of meeting and talking to strangers, I get you. That discomfort is real. But it's not an excuse. You can learn how to push past the nerves and have effective conversations that lead to the professional connections you want.

Nail down your elevator pitch and practice until you can do it in your sleep.

One of the best remedies for nervousness is preparation. A lot of the time, when people tell me they're nervous about networking, it's because they don't know what to say. They get into a room full of influential strangers, and they forget how to formulate a sentence. If this is your struggle, you need to craft and perfect your elevator pitch/personal brand statement – a sentence or two to explain what you do, why you do it, and why anyone should care. No matter how great you, your business, or your services are, if you can't quickly explain to someone why they should want anything to do with you, your business is going to forever be a hobby. When someone asks, "What do you do?" a perfected elevator pitch helps you make sure that the next thing that comes out of your mouth makes them want to learn more.

Michael Hyatt totally helped me get mine together. One of the things you want to remember is that people aren't going to be interested in connecting with someone if they can't understand what value you can add for them. So, here's the formula I got from Hyatt that I used to create my pitch:

✓ Your Professional Identity (I am)

+

✓ Target Audience (I help)

+

✓ Unique Solution (Do/Understand)

=

✓ Your specific transformation (Value added)

Here's an example of what that could sound like: "I'm a speaker, author, and mentor. I help millennial women see beyond the limits of their circumstances, so they have reason to make choices that liberate them."

See, simple, straightforward, and it's clear immediately what I do and why I do it. But preparation doesn't stop there.

A pitch doesn't come in one-size-fits-all, so be prepared to customize.

Your elevator pitch is the foundation of your conversations with potential connections, but you still need to be able to reach them personally and give them a reason why they should want to be connected to you in any capacity. I tweak my pitch for different people in different environments and you should too. That's going to take a little bit more work on your part to understand what value you can add to this person's life specifically. There are a couple of ways to do this:

1. Do a little internet creeping before you reach out.

This obviously doesn't work if they're already standing in front of you and you've never heard of them before. But if you know you'll be going into a potential networking opportunity and someone you're really interested in connecting with will be there, spend a little time scrolling their social media and reading their website content to see if they make mention of any needs or concerns you know you can address with your services. If you can speak directly to a need they've mentioned publicly and offer them a solution, you've got a much better chance of securing their interest.

2. Shut up, and listen.

Seriously, realize that networking is as much about listening as it is about talking. If you jump into conversations with people and just come out the gate blabbing about how cool you are, you're going to come off as self-centered and arrogant. Not the kind of person anyone is interested in working with. I remember going to an event and meeting an entrepreneur who was fairly well-known. I was interested in working with him and introduced myself to him with the intention of pitching him. But he radiated arrogance, and it was honestly such a turnoff. I still pitched him, but it left a sour taste in my mouth. Don't be this person. When you're talking to people, spend as much time listening as you do talking. When you let people talk, they reveal a lot of information about their interests, goals, and needs that you can then use to help you position yourself as a useful connection for them.

What it ultimately comes down to is giving people an opportunity to reveal the things they want and need, and using that to cater your pitch to them.

Now that we've helped you shake some of the jitters you might have about meeting new people, I want to circle back to what I was saying earlier about networking being something you have to actively pursue. Your pitch is useless if you never go anywhere tp get to use it. You cannot claim your dreams from the couch.

Get off your butt and go where the people are at.

Whether it's a mixer, networking event, or industry conference, you need to go out and get into the spaces where the kind of people you'd like to meet are. Don't tell me you don't know where to go. I'm not buying it. Join industry-related Facebook groups. Pay attention to the events other people in your line of business are talking about. Check out online events pages to see what's happening in your city in the next few months. Then buy your tickets and go. There are so many resources to find events, seminars, and conferences. Do some research, get into those rooms, and dare to start conversations.

But don't keep it local. Get out of your hood.

If you're an entrepreneur/business owner, I highly suggest you travel often and network while doing it. I live in Toronto, and it's one of the biggest cities in Canada, but as far as networking goes, it's so small. I can only connect with so many people here, and they can only take me so far. I love my city, but the minute I stepped outside my hood a whole world of possibilities opened up to me. I make it a point to travel for business often and attend events in the US so I can make connections there as well. I recently traveled to Washington, DC for a weekend and landed two new business deals. I organically clicked with two amazing people, and we made it happen. If I'd refused to step beyond my borders, I would have missed those opportunities. Catch flights (or buses). Plan a road trip. Just make sure that you're taking your networking beyond your city and really exploring as many possibilities for amazing connections.

I want to give a disclaimer before I drop this next piece of advice because I realize it's a risk that not everybody is willing to take, and for good reason. Let's not even call it advice. But I think that for people who are brave enough to do what I'm about to suggest, and smart enough to know when not to do it, this tip can be life-changing. You ready?

Sometimes, you have to be bold enough to crash the party.

Okay, I'm not telling you to just roll up on any event uninvited. Getting arrested for trespassing isn't cute. So, you definitely need to know when and how to pull this off. But sometimes, an opportunity presents itself (even if an invitation doesn't), and it's in your best interest to take it. I'll give you an example. A few months back, I had pitched to a tech CEO I wanted to write for. I sent him a bomb pitch email, which I saw he opened (shoutout to Hubspot for that feature), but hadn't responded to. I figured he got busy and hadn't had time to reply yet. I ended up booking a public tour of his office, not because I was planning to try to meet him necessarily, but because I thought it was a good opportunity to get a feel for him and how he operated. Turns out that the same night of the tour, his office was hosting an event to showcase a new app. I called up a friend, and we decided to attend. I ended up bumping into the founder as I was nervously practicing my pitch in the lobby. Not exactly how I'd planned to run into him, but I decided to roll with it. I spent all of six minutes speaking with him. Today, he's a client.

If I hadn't crashed the party, I don't know how long my email would have sat unanswered in his inbox. Sometimes, what it takes to convince someone that they need to connect with you is to spend some time with them face-to-face, even if it's less than ten minutes at a party you weren't invited to.

Funny enough, Bozoma Saint John, recently shared a story at the Rush Philanthropic Arts Foundation's Art for Life gala where she did something similar years ago. She snuck into a star-studded event because she knew the kind of people she wanted to rub shoulders with were going to be there. Just like me, she doesn't exactly recommend party crashing, but she does advise that you have to be confident and get yourself into rooms while, as she puts it, "you're young and dumb enough to think no one will turn you away."

But even if you never crash a celebrity party or show up at a CEO's event without an invite, make sure that you are being bold enough to network. It's not optional. Put it on your to-do list with all your other business tasks and don't skip it. Make it your mission to connect with one new person and attend relevant events at least once a month. The time you invest in building your network will pay off times a million down the road.

Andrew

I don't know if you'll find a single entrepreneur who thinks they can build a successful business without having a good network. Nobody is an island, no matter how much they want to pretend to be. You need good connections if you expect to win in a world that requires multiple pieces to come together. But to be honest, I think that most networking events are a waste of time. Generally, it's just a bunch of people handing out business cards, having awkward conversations, and hoping to get something out of it for themselves. Nine times out of ten, nothing comes out of it because a key ingredient is missing: intention.

Networking isn't something that you should just wing. That doesn't mean that it should be fake. I think genuine connections based on real conversation are best. But you shouldn't be wasting your time, or anyone else's, just talking for the sake of talking and calling it networking. If you want to build relationships and make connections that are going to be valuable for everyone involved in the long run, you need to make sure that you're putting in the work to network with a purpose. And that starts with what events you choose to go to.

You don't have to be at every networking event.

Just because an event is happening in your city doesn't mean you need to be there. You have to know if it has any real value for you. Because if you're going to be at an event where no one of interest is going to be, or you're not going to learn anything, you're better off allocating that time to something that's going to grow your business like researching, practicing creating, and learning. Stay away from happy hour events where the attendees are random. There's no way to prepare. To network intentionally, it's better if the event is relevant to your industry and you're able to research the guest list and decide who you'd like to speak with before you show up.

Don't wear yourself out trying to talk to twenty people.

Your goal shouldn't be to talk to as many people as possible in hopes of making as many connections as you can. If you try to talk to everyone in the room, you're going to spread yourself thin trying to give too many people your attention and energy. Once you've peeped the guestlist and done a little creeping to figure out who you want to connect with, keep the list short. That way you can be properly prepared for a few conversations that will be effective.

If you get caught unprepared, find the people who are staying low-key.

At every networking event, there's that one person that's the center of attention because they're loud and all over the place talking to everybody. That is not your target. Fact is, the loudest person in the room is usually the most broke with the least to offer and the most requests. Think about it. People who "really got it" are not extra or needy for more attention. They know they're good and would rather build organically than force a situation to happen for their own benefit. Don't get caught up. When I go to networking events, I hang back and observe so I can spot the other low-key people in the room who look like they're moving with intention. That's how Pauleanna and I met. We were at the Forward conference, and we both noticed that we came in with an agenda and weren't trying to be flashy. Once we spoke, we knew we were on the same wavelength, and we've now created a business partnership that benefits both of us.

Too many options honestly sucks. It's hard to tell who is real and who is not. I'd rather just meet 2-3 people and see if there's long-term growth. When you have to figure that out between 12 or more, you'll realize most people have their own selfish desires, and it becomes a huge waste of your time, dollars, and coffee beans.

I know I've been a bit critical of social media in the last couple of chapters, but I think that for networking, it can definitely be useful, and you should take advantage of the daily access it gives you to amazing people.

We've heard this way too many times, but it really does go down in the DMs.

If you're using your social media right, you should be following people you want to connect with and paying attention to the things they post on the regular. You know what they're interested, what moves they're trying to make, what struggles they might have shared on the timeline. Use that to your advantage and slide into their DMs to let them know you see them, you've got a solution, and you'd love to connect. The key to making connections online work is consistency and leverage. Whatever you have that that contact may want—skills, network, talents, services, even time—be prepared to use it to offer them value. This gives you the leverage you need to initiate a conversation they'd be willing to engage in. But don't just message once and drop it. Be consistent with your engagement and follow up to nurture that connection and stay at the front of their mind. If you work it right, a DM can be the start of a solid business relationship.

Social media is also very helpful for this next networking tip. Next time you're considering a networking opportunity, shift your approach. Derek Coburn is the founder of Cadre an exclusive mastermind community. He's also the author of Networking is not Working, and in his book, he asks us to change the way we think about networking. He calls it Networking 3.0, and it kinda flips networking as we know it on its head by asking people to network for others instead of themselves.

Upgrade your relationship building game by practicing Networking 3.0.

Typically, networking has worked in one of two ways. We either ask people what they can do for us (Networking 1.0), or we try to persuade people of what we can do for them (Networking 2.0). Neither one of those is the worst thing in the world, and I think a lot of the advice we've offered already has been Networking 2.0. But it's also good to consider how we can tap our network to help others. That is Networking 3.0. The idea is to think about how the person you're talking to could be a good connection for someone you know, like a client. Instead of just focusing on you getting a direct return, you pass on the referral and help someone else out. It's a win-win because your client gets a valuable connection, and you build up goodwill with a client who will be more inclined to swing referrals your way because you were considerate of them too.

Whatever networking practices you use, remember that like any other business practice, networking is a long game. Not every connection you make is going to have instant pay off. Sometimes months, or even years, may go by before something comes out of a business relationship. Don't stress. Just make sure you're still nurturing those relationships. Stay connected, check in periodically, and show interest in the things they're doing, even if it's not something you can help with directly. The point is to build a relationship, not to plot for a transaction. If you focus on fostering a relationship, when the time comes, the opportunities and benefits will be clear.

PAIR UP TO LEVEL UP

Andrew

Once you've started securing some cool connections and the relationships feel solid, your next thought is probably how you can work with some of these people to make something cool happen. There are tons of ways you can do this. You could do brand partnerships, collaborations, influencer marketing, business partnerships, a co-branded product, co-hosted events, guest appearances on blogs, YouTubes, and podcasts, brand sponsorship, social media account takeovers. The possibilities just depend on what kind of relationship you've built and what everybody has to bring to the table. If you're considering tapping one of your relationships to work together, you have to start by knowing what you can do for each other.

Lay everything out and see what comes up.

Before you do any collaboration, everyone involved needs to be clear about what they have to offer and how it could benefit the others and the goal they're hoping to achieve. For example, when Pauleanna and I decided to collab on BYOB Society and this book, I knew that she was a strong writer, a solid entrepreneur with three successful brands, a great network, and a loyal following. I brought branding expertise, a decade of entrepreneurial experience, and a platform that was already in the works. We both had things that would be helpful to each other, so a partnership just made sense. But things aren't always so even. When you have less to offer, you have to take a different approach.

If you ain't got the leverage, Sway, you may have to give to get.

I've been speaking for almost five years now. But when I started, I wasn't great. I used to be sweaty and terrified of speaking to a crowd. Stage fright is a serious thing. But I kept at it. At the time, I was eager to build experience and establish myself as a thought leader and expert in my space. So, I did hundreds of gigs in cities across the US. All completely free. I knew that the depth of my speaking could only go as far as the depth of my knowledge and speaking for free really gave me time and space to grow and develop in my business and as a speaker.

Now, because I've put in the work and offer enough value, organizations are willing to pay me to speak to their audiences and my speaking schedule is starting to look like a pro's. I'm earning four-figure checks for gigs which blows my mind because five years ago, I couldn't have imagined accepting a check to get up on a stage.

The thing is, leverage takes time. I know everybody wants to get paid or see big returns when they work with other people. But here's a big key, you will always get less than what you're worth, as a student, employee, or entrepreneur. Seriously, drill this into your head, and you won't be upset anymore when someone doesn't meet your expectations. They usually don't. It's natural for you to feel like you're worth more. You know you, but other people don't, so they won't give all of them for all of you. That's why timing and relationship-building are so important, it helps the other party know more about you, which builds a deeper relationship and both parties become willing to give more to each other. Time, time, time is the game we're really playing. It's un-scalable but, my goodness, it's the secret to success.

We all want to turn a profit. But sometimes, when you're fresh on a scene and don't have as much to offer as others, working for free has payoffs that go way beyond a check. For me, it was the experience and growth. For you, it might be connections, skills, or opportunities. Sometimes, it's just about the humility of realizing that the goal of changing lives and improving the world doesn't always need to have a dollar value attached.

If you are in a position to partner or collab with another person or brand where you're more on par, make sure you cover your back and ensure the partnership is mutually beneficial. I've had four partnerships and collaborations just fall completely flat because I didn't have all the things in place that were necessary to make sure things would work. So, here's an opportunity to learn from my mistakes:

Business partnerships are like dating relationships. Compatibility matters.

It's like if you met a beautiful person, and they had all the things you were looking for. That checklist you had for the perfect bae? They checked every box. And then you get together, and it's like you don't even know who they are. It's a whole mess, and everybody loses. The same principle applies to partnerships and collabs. Even if the brand or person you're looking to work with has all the things that would make your project perfect, if when you work together, there's always friction, and you can't agree on any suggestions or plans, none of the other stuff is going to matter. So, test your partnerships first, especially if you're talking a full-fledged business partner or co-founder. Make sure that your business philosophies, values, and approaches play well together and work on a small project and see how that goes. If things feel off, trust your gut and let it go.

There are no free rides. Make sure everybody is pulling their weight.

Let's use this relationship analogy again because it's so perfect. If you've ever been in a relationship where one person is trying more than the other, you know how fast that gets to be a problem. The same thing will happen in your business partnerships if one party isn't holding up their end of their bargain. A business partner who slacks off on duties, an influencer who doesn't post what they promised, an event co-host who forgets to book a vendor. Just some of the nightmares that could happen in one-sided partnerships. If there's slacking, call it out in the beginning and move on if things don't improve.

Get the to-do lists super clear.

All the disaster scenarios that I described above can happen if people aren't clear about who's supposed to do what. So, over-communicate until someone tells you not to. Make sure that before anything gets moving, everybody is clear about what they're supposed to be doing. This way, all the responsibilities get covered by the person who's best for the job.

When you get this stuff right, the collaborations can be so awesome. Despite the partners I had that didn't work out, I've had collabs and partnerships that were amazing for everyone involved. Don't be afraid to look in your network for people you can work with, just make sure that you're taking steps to get the most out of working together.

Pauleanna

With so many options for collaboration, there's really no excuse not to connect and work with other brands. In fact, I don't know a successful business who does not collab or partner with another. If you run a company/brand, you need to master the art of the pitch or hire someone on your team who can do it correctly. There's an art to it (and a lot of prayer, bruh). But it's doable.

I regularly pitch to brands and companies whose work and missions I admire. I easily spend two or three hours crafting each pitch, but it's worth the time because those carefully written emails have helped me land partnerships that have really boosted my brand.

If you want to collab with someone in your network, perfect your approach and go for it.

I recently reached out to a c-level executive and raised my hand. I started a conversation around a few elements that were missing in her personal brand and offered to help (expecting nothing in return.) I admire this individual so much. The chance to brainstorm with her was a dream come true. No dollar value could compare. I genuinely wanted to help position her into the powerhouse I know she is. To show her I was serious, I even jumped on a plane, flew to her office and did another pitch in person, this time with a detailed presentation specifically outlining how my skills and expertise can benefit her platform.

Do not be intimidated by titles, if you are cool, smart, interesting, and offer value, they will listen. Even the busiest and most successful people in the world are open to listening to you if you help solve a problem, not create more of them. I fulfilled a need. My contribution will save her time. I strategically planned out how we can achieve her desired result and she hired me on the spot. This exec is now one of my biggest clients. The most important question you need to ask when you're preparing your approach is to find the problem your business, brand, or skills can solve. That's what's going to keep your email out of the spam folder. Never approach with an ask that doesn't add value. That's not a collab, it's a favor. Always be prepared to add value and solve a problem.

Turn online connections into offline collaborations.

The primary reason I use social media is to build brand awareness and connect with cool, smart and interesting people. For instance, New Jersey City University Professor Lenny Williams. I first came across Lenny on Instagram. I'm a very observant person, so when I see a leader, I pay close attention. Lenny has many attractive qualities. He is intelligent, a community activist and uses his story to empower others. We started out as strangers, but after I reached out on IG, he quickly became like a brother to me.

As we chatted more about business and learned about each other's platforms, we got excited about the idea of collaborating. So, when Lenny came over from Jersey to Toronto, we got together and put on a workshop and taught a class of young dreamers how to proceed without permission and turn opposition into opportunity.

Don't hesitate to take your coolest online relationships offline through awesome collaborations. Whether that means someone flies out or you meet in the middle, it's worth the time, money and effort it takes to connect with your favorite social media friends to create something that will benefit both your brands.

Online connects become so much more powerful when you take them off the web and into the real world.

Don't just work with friends. Turn competitors into collaborators too.

In the Toronto speaking market, there are quite a few women who speak on a lot of the same topics that I do. Technically, they're my competition, but I try to find opportunities to work with them instead of against them. My girl Chivon John is a wellness advocate who does a fair amount of public speaking. We could be competitors, but we chose to be friends, and it's been great for both of us. She and I have worked together on quite a few projects, including a wellness workshop for women, a vision board pajama party, and most recently, we co-founded Mogul Talk, a mastermind group for millennial entrepreneurs. Realize that people who are in the same lane as you might be able to help you along your journey if you learn to see them as potential collaborators instead of constantly trying to compete with them.

When you're first starting out, a lot of your focus is going to be on collaboration from the position of giving or partnering. But when opportunities to have your needs met come up, don't be shy about taking them.

When a contact says, "How can I help?" Ask big and be specific.

Chances are if they're asking what they can do for you, they're genuinely willing to help you out. Believe me, I understand the urge to downplay your request. But let me tell you a story to help you see why I've left that mentality behind. Back in 2015, I went to New York to see one of my mentors who works at the ESSENCE Magazine head office. She had featured me in the January 2015 issue, and I wanted to bring her a copy of my novel and thank her personally.

As we were chatting, she asked me, "How can I help you? Tell me what it is you want." I felt apprehensive to ask for too much since I had already been published in the magazine. So, I replied and asked her if she could push my book to any of her media friends as the 2-year anniversary was coming up.

She's usually a sweet, soft-spoken person, but she glared me and said, "Girl, you are sitting in the office of ESSENCE Magazine, and you're asking me to connect you to a blogger?"

We both laughed, but she got serious and told me that I should always be specific with my ask whether it be in my prayers, to my friends, family, a business contact—whoever. So, I did. I cleared my throat and confidently asked to be blessed with another feature. She said yes and connected me with one of her editors.

When you get the chance, ask big and be specific because you will only receive blessings on the level of your requirements.

No matter what kind of collaboration you undertake though, there's one thing you absolutely need to do.

Get an airtight contract to cover your butt and your business.

As my brand and businesses grow, it's extremely important that I keep my paperwork very well organized. Every time I make any kind of collaborative arrangement, I make sure to have a contract in place. This goes hand-in-hand with Andrew's advice to make sure that roles and duties are clearly defined, and everyone knows what they're expecting to get from the collaboration. A contract makes sure that if those arrangements come into question later, you've got a document that can clear up any confusion.

One of the biggest mistakes I made as a newbie entrepreneur is that there was no paperwork. Contracts? Ha! I was juggling so much on a shaky foundation which left me overwhelmed and stressed, and to add to the mess, I didn't have any contracts in place to protect the work and effort I was hustling to get done. I was being counterproductive by not having certain legal documents in place when establishing business partnerships and collaborations.

That's not a mistake I'll make again, and you shouldn't either. What I did was register for resources like Small Business Bodyguard, a legal service by Rachel Rodgers who is a business lawyer and intellectual property strategist, to learn how to cover my bases, my assets, and my ass. Make sure you do the work to protect yourself as well. Collabs are amazing, but be smart about it.

Chapter 16:
Think Bigger

───── ⊙✛⊙ ─────

REINVENTED CLASSICS

───── ⊙✛⊙ ─────

Andrew

We've all heard that quote about the definition of insanity. You know, doing the same thing over and over expecting different results. I don't know for sure that that makes you insane, but it definitely doesn't make you smart. Yet, somehow people keep pushing persistence as the key to entrepreneurial success. That's not it. Don't get me wrong, I'm not saying that being a good entrepreneur doesn't require the ability to keep pushing when things get hard. But the kind of persistence I'm warning you against is the stubborn, hard-headed kind that will just keep doing the same thing a thousand times, and won't even think about switching up no matter how many times it fails.

One of the biggest things I'm changing up on is instead of telling people what they should do, I simply give my two cents and let it go. Because, honestly, most won't listen. They're just too stubborn until they go through their own experiences and then truly understand what's real and what's not. I've been mentoring and helping folks for ten years. Trust me, I know this is a true statement. I always tell people if you don't humble yourself, life will do it for you. Sad part is it hurts so much more the longer you wait, but we've all been there, and that's what keeps me humble more than ever before. I don't want to think I know everything or have all the answers because as soon as I get big-headed and stubborn, it all comes crashing down.

It's like a labyrinth or maze. If you find a different direction, don't just keep slamming your head through the brick wall because you told yourself that's the path you want to take. That's stupid. If you think you're the Hulk Hogan of business and can break down the wall, then kudos to you. But stubborn persistence as a business approach makes no sense at all. So, when people say things like "Keep pushing" and "Don't quit," all I can think is, "Damn, that's terrible advice." If you keep pushing at the thing that flopped the first 99 times, it's probably gonna flop the hundredth time too. I was chatting with Regina Anaejionu, the blogging guru, and she said, "With pretty much any business idea there is a way to arrive at a profitable business model within that, but it is not always the first thing that comes to your mind." She's right. So, don't quit, pivot and grow.

Learn to turn on a dime.

Even the best entrepreneurs hit roadblocks or have flat out failures. Sir James Dyson, the dude who created those amazing bagless vacuum cleaners that barely make a whisper, he had 5,126 prototypes that failed before he got the design right. The founder of Hershey's chocolate had three candy companies fail before he created the company we all know today. Even Jeff Bezos, the founder of Amazon, literally the world's biggest online retailer, had business ideas flop. What they all have in common is that when shit went south, they figured out how to change directions and try something different.

If you're struggling with a business idea that just isn't coming together, it's time to pivot. Pivoting is a popular term for startups and growing businesses because it refers to a business' ability to shift its strategy when necessary. The reality is, your business will probably change from your original plan. Issues are going to come up that you might never have imagined. You're going to stumble across questions you don't have the answers to. Sometimes, things are just going to fall apart no matter how hard you try to make them work. Pivoting successfully in these cases is about figuring out how to change direction in a way that solves the problem and keeps you ahead of the game.

Use the facts to set your course.

When you realize that the direction you originally chose isn't going to work and you need to pivot, you're going to have to use the facts and all the info you can find to help you make your decision. Carefully examine your business from the top down to figure out what's broken then start doing research to figure out how to fix it. What exactly you'll have to research will depend on your business and the problem you're facing. But I'm willing to bet that if you dig a little and ask the right people, you can find some of the answers you need to figure out what needs to be tweaked, changed, or tossed out. Once you get it figured out, sit on it a bit.

Don't be reactive. Give your ideas time to brew.

I'm a big believer in failing fast and failing forward, but I'm not about rushing. When you've pinpointed where you need to pivot, and you start making plans to execute the switch up, you need to take the time to assess your new idea to see if it will really help you solve the issue you were dealing with before. Pivoting is about making the next best move, and you can't know you're doing that unless you properly test out that move.

Sometimes pivoting isn't about fixing an issue, but just upgrading a part of your brand that already exists. There is a term called trend slacking. A new business basically takes a few different trends to make their new product/service unique. This is a great strategy.

Because everybody loves an upgrade.

There are a lot of ways you can approach this. You just need to take an honest look at your business and figure out what could use some refreshing. Here are some things you can do to give your brand a facelift. If your brand has evolved a bit, a logo switch-up or website redesign could be a good look. If a product anniversary is coming up, do a relaunch with dope new packaging, kinda like Pauleanna did when she re-released her novel with a new cover. Take some time to flesh out the idea for a service or product that has been keeping you up at night and drop something new on the market. That's pretty much how BYOB Society came to be. You've got options, you just have to figure out what's a good look for you and your brand.

The important thing to remember is that no business is perfect the first time around. It can be for any number of reasons—unexpected issues, changing markets, competitors make moves, technology improvements. Even if there's no drastic issue, every business will always have room for growth and improvement. Businesses that thrive are the ones that understand how to pivot when they need to.

INNOVATION IN THE AGE OF EXPERIENCE

Pauleanna

How do people feel when they work with you? The answer to that question matters more now than ever before. Yes, winning over a customer base has always been about ensuring that the customer walks away from your business feeling great. But there's been a shift in business where customers don't just want a service or product—they want an amazing experience. When they feel like they're not getting that, they move on. Unless you're the only person in the world doing exactly what you do, if you leave your customers hanging, they're going to find someone else to get their services from. So, you need to make sure that every customer who hits your site or walks through your doors feels like they're working with the best because good experiences create loyalty.

Don't let your marketing be false advertising. You can spend thousands claiming how great your product or service is, but if people aren't having a good customer experience working with you, your marketing budget is just a waste of cash. You need to deliver amazing customer service if you want people to choose you over anybody else.

Don't just promise greatness, be great.

A company that totally nails this is Zappos. I swear Tony Hsieh is a genius. Zappos sells shoes online. There are a ton of companies you can order shoes from, but Zappos has consistently stood out as the go-to, and it's because their customer service is top notch. They've got a simple and easy to use website, their site has diverse and interesting content, your shopping experience is personalized to you, and when you have a problem, you can get someone on the phone to help you out. Seriously, go Google Zappos and customer service to see the way people rave about this company.

If you want to move product or book clients and get people invested in your brand, you need to make customer service a priority. Make sure that when they need help, you've got the answers, have your bases covered when it comes to invoicing, be genuinely apologetic when you make mistakes and make sure you resolve issues when they come up.

Customer service doesn't end when the invoice is paid.

Don't make the mistake of thinking the customer experience starts and ends with the sale. So many businesses focus on the marketing and closing the sale, but once they've got the customer's money in their pocket, they stop caring. This is a bad move if you want customers to stay loyal to your business.

There's an amazing video by Joey Coleman on YouTube called 'The First 100 Days.' He explains that most businesses lose 20-30% of their customers within the first 100 days because there's nothing being done to retain the customer after the sale has been secured. He gives great tips on how to continue catering to your customer to keep them on board, including things like follow-up emails to see how they're enjoying the service, emails with how-to videos to encourage them to use the product, or discount codes or gifts to thank them for their purchase. The goal is to show them you care about them beyond the invoice. This is especially true if you have a service-based business. Don't let your clients feel ghosted. Update them and keep in touch

Get personal.

As a small business, you have the advantage of being able to connect personally with customers in ways that big corporations can't. Chances are your customers or clients have interacted with you directly at one point or another. If you learn how to maximize that personal connection between your brand and your clients, you can pretty much ensure that they'll stay loyal to your brand.

Of course, your business is going to have systems and processes in place that all your customers go through, but make sure that you don't take that one-size-fits-all strategy too far. Use the fact that you know who your customers are to cater to them as individuals. For me, I'm always thinking about how I can make every one of my clients' experiences better. For both my mentees and my writing clients, I put their name on a board, and I'm constantly brainstorming ways to make them feel good.

You should do this too. Some simple ideas you can consider are custom videos for people on special occasions, handwritten notes of appreciation or encouragement, or celebrating client anniversaries with a card or a small gift. The key is to let every client know that you see them and their needs individually. If you make people feel special, they'll stick with you forever.

Be delightful.

Honestly, sometimes it's not what you do but how you do it. Shawn Johnson says, "You have to delight every opportunity you get. Every time you get to shake a hand, make an introduction you have to build on people's wonderment of what is possible." I totally agree. If it were all about what you did, there would be no reason why your customer would choose you over someone else who sells the same product or offers the service you do. It's the little things you do to impress and delight your customer that make that difference.

I'll give you an example. When I first started out with my business, I worked with an amazing Toronto photographer named Samantha Clarke. Everything about working with her was so dope. In every consultation, she was totally present and made sure she understood my vision. On shoot day, she gave me directions to help me get the money shot. But something I really loved was that when she delivered the photos after a shoot, she gave them to me on a custom USB in a cute box with her logo on it. It always felt like such a nice touch on top of already great service.

Always think of what you can do to make your customer feel excited about working with you. It could be unique packaging, small gifts or tokens of appreciation, newsletters that are full of info and opportunities that are exciting and relevant to your customer base. Take some time to figure out the kinds of things that would make your client happy and then give it to them.

One thing I don't want you to forget with all these bells and whistles is to make sure that your product or service itself is top notch.

Don't forget the main course.

Ultimately, your customers came to you because they wanted what you had to offer. They wanted you to help them solve a problem or fulfill a need. Yes, the trimmings like gifts and cute packaging are great, but they won't compensate for a sloppy product or service. Ultimately, if you do nothing else, do good work, and do it on time.

GETTING YOUR TEAM TOGETHER

Pauleanna

No one is self-made.

At some point in our lives, we've had to stand on the shoulders of giants. My "giants" are mentors, my parents, my pastor, and my staff, the team of amazing people I work with every single day. Getting to the point of having a staff I could depend on to help me grow was a work in progress, though. When I started my first business eight years ago, I couldn't even tell you the definition of a brand, much more how to effectively manage staff.

But over time, I came to understand that I didn't know everything, and I didn't need to. I just needed to surround myself with people who are smarter than me and good at what they do. My hiring decisions have always revolved around my weaknesses. That's why I currently manage a team of 22 freelancers across all my businesses who excel at their skills. Managing them is just a matter of letting them know my vision and what needs to be done and trusting them to execute. And they come through every time.

If you're in need of the support that having the right staff can bring, I encourage you to make that move.

Make your first hires people who do something you can't do that your business can't live without.

I don't hire just to have bodies around. I hire to meet my organizations' needs. Some of the first people I hired were brought on when I was making big moves in my business that I never had before. In those cases, they weren't necessarily long-term hires, but they were very needed at the time. As my writing and speaking career took off and I wanted to secure press opportunities, I hired a publicist. I hired a website designer when I was switching over from my little blogspot.com site to a proper platform. When I was publishing my book, I had an event planner take care of the book launch. They all came on board to help me with things that were essential that I simply didn't have the skillset for at the time. Working with them wasn't cheap, but hiring isn't about bargain shopping. It's about investing in the best possible work for your business.

There's a time and reason for making more permanent hires too. While web development and event planning aren't things I need for my business every day, there were other tasks that mattered for day-to-day operation that I wanted help with. And the more I grew, the more help I needed. Juggling everything became out of the question. As your business expands, you'll find this too. Don't burn out trying to do it all and be it all.

As you grow, narrow your focus, and get staff on board to handle the rest.

When there's too much on your plate, and you need to accommodate your growth, hiring lets you replicate yourself. My assistant has always been one of the most important hires for me because they take on a lot of the admin stuff that allows me to focus on other parts of my business. I can chase leads, pitch huge clients, and catch flights to close deals because I have an assistant running things in the background for me. Whether it's an assistant, an accountant, a receptionist, or a partner, make sure you're hiring people who can take care of the task as well as you, if not better.

As your team grows, you may discover that elements are missing that you might not even have expected.

Hire people who are good enough to fill the gaps.

I have a team of brilliant writers for my content writing firm, WritersBlok. Some of them are amazing at op-eds, others write killer speeches. Books, press releases, marketing materials, copywriting—we've got it all covered. So, when one of my latest WritersBlok hires slid into my inbox looking to join the team, I was ready to tell her, "Nah, we're good." But something told me to give her a chance. She's a solid writer, but where she really shines is with data. She's so good at research and turning information into something we can really work with. She brought a strength to the team that no one else had. When you're looking to hire, seek out gems like these. People who bring unique strengths and skills to the table will ensure that your team is well-rounded, and all bases are covered.

No matter what position you hire for, always make sure that you're seeking out people who are a good fit for your team. No matter how amazing a person's credentials and resume are, if they don't fit your team or get your vision, it's not going to work.

Trust your gut and hire based on the culture you want for your business.

I honestly don't even look at resumes. Before I hire someone, I have a conversation and trust the gut feeling I get when I speak with them. Because my gut never steers me wrong. All my teammates are ninjas. We move swift and silent. Work ethic on 1,000. I expect everyone on my team to be innovative, flexible, and willing to step up to the plate. Sometimes, a piece of paper can't convey if someone can meet that. I need to see and hear people to understand if they're going to fit in with the culture.

There are rare occasions where a resume really blows my mind. I haven't necessarily had anything like this come across my desk, but I remember seeing the Francine for Spotify campaign created by Francine Tamakloe, a young woman who answered Spotify's job posting with a personalized website resume that showcased her knowledge of the company, her relevant interests and skills, and the experience that made her a good fit. Her extra effort landed her the job. Of course, I'm not expecting people who want to work with me to do all this—though I'd be impressed as hell—but I'm always interested in people who are willing to go the extra mile to join the team, because I know they'll give their everything once they're on board.

Of course, not every person who's interested in working for you is going to wow you. And sometimes you might hire someone, and they might not be quite what you need. Some people, no matter how eager they are, are just not going to be right for the role, or your business altogether.

Don't be afraid to turn down applications and fire bad fits.

I've had to deal with both. Over the years, I've had staff members I hired on who were amazing when they started but, as time passed, things started to go downhill. They were distracted, late to meetings, disappearing frequently. The work wasn't up to par. I struggled because they were extremely skilled and great when they were on point. Sometimes it was that they simply outgrew the position or that they had another dream to follow and they'd fallen out of love with the job. It was a challenge, but I had to let them go. There were no hard feelings. It was just the best decision for my business. I take the same approach with people who apply, but either don't have what I need or don't feel like a good fit. I'm gentle but honest with them about why I'm saying no, but I say no.

Your business is your baby and you have to be able to trust every member of your staff will help you keep it going. There is no room for people who aren't giving their best or meeting your standards. Always prioritize your business and its needs.

Don't let the thought of having to fire staff or reject applicants discourage you. Hiring staff and building a team is a challenge, but it's necessary for your growth. If it's time to expand your team, then do it. Spend the funds and make the leap. Even if you come across some people you don't connect with, keep it pushing and try again until you get it right.

Andrew

For a lot of entrepreneurs, the business starts out with a staff of one—aka you. Whatever work needs to be done, we get it handled. It means a lot of sleepless nights and figuring out how to get things done, but we make it happen. But it's nearly impossible for a business to grow with just one person taking care of everything. You can only do so much. And at some point, if you're trying to do it all by yourself, you're going to drop the ball on something.

When things start to feel crazy overwhelming like that, the next thought is usually, "Man, I need some help," and the question of hiring full-time staff comes up. If you're at this point, it means you're probably growing, and that's a good thing. But the answer may not be to get staff.

You shouldn't hire just because you need help.

Hiring is a big decision, and sometimes it's a necessary one, but it's not always the right choice. You shouldn't hire unless you know what kind of help you need. If you're feeling stressed and overwhelmed, hiring someone just because, without having defined tasks or duties for them to do isn't going to solve any problems. Now you're just spending money, and you still have the stress of figuring out how to deal with how overwhelmed you are. You also shouldn't hire someone just because they said they could help when you mentioned a problem. Hiring isn't something you rush into because if you bring the wrong person into your business, they could sink the whole thing.

For most beginners who are strapped on resources, you should be hiring for three reasons:

1. You need a specific thing done regularly.

Anyone you hire should have a specific role to play in your business. And it should be something you need done on a daily, weekly, or monthly basis. If it's something you need once in a blue moon, you can contract that out. If you're going to be putting someone on your payroll, they need to be worth that bi-weekly check.

2. You're going to get back a return on the investment.

Hiring needs to make sense from a financial standpoint. If you're paying someone money to do something for you, but in the long run it doesn't make your business more money, I wouldn't call that money well spent. A hire needs to make you more money than they cost you.

3. This person can do something you can't. Or at least better than you.

There's no point in passing a task to someone else unless they're going to do it better and faster than you. The point of hiring is to get things done, take them off your plate, and free up time for you to focus on the things you're good at. But if you're going to find yourself taking care of the task yourself because you're just better at it, or cleaning up behind a staff member who does a sloppy job, you're not saving yourself any trouble.

If you're still trying to figure out if you should be hiring and you're stuck, it's time to do the research. I guarantee you that you're not the only person who's been in the spot you're in right now, trying to figure out if they need to start hiring. So, hit up Google.

Find out how other bosses in your industry handled the hiring dilemma.

Check sites like Forbes, Entrepreneur, Inc, and Business Insider and read the articles that talk about hiring. Go to the library and pick up a book about business and entrepreneurship and find the chapter on hiring. Ask mentors and other people in your industry and line of business what they did at your stage and how they handled hiring. Who was their first employee and what did they do? You don't have to figure it out by yourself. The answers exist. You just need to dig a little.

If you've sat down and really assessed your business and the help you need, and it turns out you do need to hire, you're probably trying to figure out if you can afford to hire a staff member. As a small business in the early stages, especially if you're self-funding, this can be a bit of a hurdle. You don't want to hire someone who isn't really qualified just because that's the only person you can afford to pay.

Stretch your budget by hiring smart instead of cheap.

There are laws about full-time employees that require you to pay benefits and paid vacation and other technical costs that can really add up. If you just can't foot that kind of cost right now, you've got options. You could hire contractors and freelancers and just pay them by the project or a monthly retainer fee. Another option is interns. Internships can either be unpaid or done for a set fee that's usually lower than a standard salary. Put out a call for interns — social media is great for this — and see if you can find someone with quality work who has great skills and is eager to build experience.

Hiring is inevitable. At least if you plan to have any real success in your business. But don't rush into it. Every person you hire can directly impact your brand for better or for worse, and you don't want to take the chance of bringing on someone that puts what you've built at risk. Hire slow and hire smart.

Chapter 17:
Wealth and Well-Being

·········· ⚜ ··········

MENTAL MOMENT

·········· ⚜ ··········

Pauleanna

I love being an entrepreneur. Everything we talk about in this book is genuinely exciting for me. Like, I really love this shit. But I also recognize that the life that comes along with it is heavy. Entrepreneurship has a psychological price, and I wouldn't feel right if I didn't talk about it transparently here. Building a business from the ground up and keeping it operating successfully comes with a lot of pressure, and it's easy for just about anybody to crumble under that if they're not careful. A Forbes article found that common mental health issues for entrepreneurs include depression, anxiety, addiction, and self-worth issues.

For me, this is all so real. I struggled with these issues before I became an entrepreneur and I have to be very intentional as I run my businesses to ensure that they don't swallow me now. I'm sure there are some of you reading this who are battling with mental health right now, and others who may be just starting to feel the weight. I would hate to see any of you fail at your dreams because your mental wellness took a back seat for too long.

So, when I say that I want everyone who is building a brand to take care of their mental health, I mean that very seriously. We all want to create amazing businesses, but burnout, depression, and overwhelming stress isn't the price we should have to pay for it.

I've spent a lot of time working on my mental strength. It's a journey I'm still figuring out. It takes a lot of work, and for me that includes self-love rituals, detailed morning routines, the occasional social media break, a lot of talk therapy, and Seinfeld. I need reruns of Seinfeld. It makes me laugh, and we all know laughter is the best medicine. I realize that the specific things that help me take care of my mind so I can chase my goals may not work for everyone. There is no secret sauce, magic fairy dust, or easy street. I encourage you, as you work on developing your business and protecting its growth, that you also work developing ways to take care of your mental health too. Here are some of the things I do that might help you figure out where to start.

Break from the grind for a minute or two.

If you're feeling burnt out or depressed and struggling to keep pushing, it's a good move to switch things up and do something different. My new routines include working out with my neighbor, grabbing coffee with old friends, playing with my Godchildren, journaling, coloring in coloring books, taking classes like improv or dance, spending time with the young women I mentor. It's important to remember that you're human, and you need to find time to do things that remind you of that.

Speak your affirmations.

As entrepreneurs, we're going to struggle with fear of failure. The stats say it's more likely than not. Every little mess-up can feel monumental. The pressure to succeed when we don't have a plan B is insane. You need to make sure you're countering all the messages that make you feel discouraged. I love affirmations, and I have one for almost every circumstance. If you were to walk into my room, the first thing you'd see is sticky notes. Tons of them. They're on the walls, the mirror, the door and inside my closet; all reminders of the woman I am becoming and the empire I'm building.

I give myself some credit.

With so much noise going on around me, at times, I place too much focus on what I still have to achieve and experience emotions that leave me feeling like I don't measure up. I lose sight of what I have already accomplished and count myself out of the game. But then I look around my room, flip through my scrapbook, or dial up a friend, and I'm reminded of how far I've come. I'm reminded that although it took a million baby steps to get here, the fact is, I am still standing which means I am getting better every day.

I have stopped trying to please everyone.

This is something I quit many years ago. The day I dropped out of school is the day I broke free from labels, naysayers and the expectations of others. Of course, I'm human, and there are times when people talk, and I admit I get sad for a few moments. But then it hits me that I have to just do me. I am on this path, and unless they've been in my shoes, most will never understand. So, I pick and choose my battles and have learned that the only opinion that matters is the one I have about myself.

Recognize that prioritizing you sets the foundation for your success.

Listen, no business or dollar value is more important than your mental health. If I need a social media timeout, I take it. If I need to book an appointment to see my doctor, I call him. If I need a personal day from work or business, I put people in place to keep things running while I take that break. Whatever move I have to make to make positivity louder and my health better, I do that. I know there's a fear that if we step back from our businesses for more than a minute, it will all fail. And, to be fair, if you're a new founder, taking a long vaca might be out of the question, but you can take a day. Make it happen.

The simple fact is, before you can achieve anything in life, you have to get your mental health in order. It's an issue that is swept under the rug and not openly discussed nearly enough. Entrepreneurs take on a 'fake it till you make it' attitude, but while we're ignoring our issues, we're putting our businesses at risk of failing, and ourselves at risk of falling apart. We need to take time to think about it and to put things in place that will keep us going. Identify your triggers and experiment with different coping mechanisms to find out what works best for you.

NOTES

MEET OUR EXPERTS

We want you to be able to follow and connect with the awesome people we referenced throughout this book, so here are their names and where you can find them online.

Alexandra Elle	@alex_elle
Alex Wolf	@alexwolf
Angela Rye	@angelarye
Ashley Chea	@watermeloneggrolls
Bea Arthur	@bbarthur
Bozoma Saint John	@badassboz
Charreah Jackson	@charreah
Courtney Sanders	@thinkngrowchick
Dana Chanel	@danachanel
Dana Falsetti	@nolatrees
Danielle Laporte	@daniellelaporte
Eric Thomas	@etthehiphoppreacher
Gary Vaynerchuk	@garyvee
John Henry	@johnhenrystyle
Karen Civil	@karencivil
Kevin Matthew	@mayorofoctober
Lisa Nichols	@lisa2motivate
Marie Forleo	@marieforleo
Michael Hyatt	@michaelhyatt
Rakia Reynolds	@rakiareynolds
Regina Anajienou	@byreginatv
Shannae Ingleton	@torontoshay
Shannon Boodram	@shanboody
Shawn Johnson	@digitalsleep
Tim Ferriss	@timferriss
Tola Lawal	@tolaspeakstome
Tony Robbins	@tonyrobbins
Vashtie Kola	@vashtie
Sheldon Neil	@sheldonneil

Pauleanna Reid
- AUTHOR -

Pauleanna Reid is the co-founder of New Girl on the Block, a mentorship platform for millennial women who are dealing with major life and career transitions. Her passions include advocacy for anti-bullying and mental health to which she contributes her time spreading awareness, providing expertise on media platforms, and delivering keynote talks in schools nationwide. When she is not working with young adults, she is growing her brand as a professional writer. She previously released a novel, Everything I Couldn't Tell My Mother, in 2014. Today, Pauleanna has successfully crafted a business in storytelling as a journalist, author, and celebrity ghostwriter. She lives in Toronto, Canada. Follow her journey online at **@pauleannareid**.

Andrew Nguyen
- AUTHOR -

Andrew Nguyen is an innovator, brand builder, and the co-founder of The O Agency: A Brand and Performance Marketing agency that services a diverse roster of all-star NFL and NBA athletes, Fortune 500 companies, and SMBs. He also helps hundreds of up-and-coming entrepreneurs each month with free trainings, consultations, connections, and more through his online platform byobsociety.com. A proud graduate of Hampton University and a member of Alpha Phi Alpha Fraternity Incorporated, Nguyen regularly speaks coast to coast as a way to give back and inspire the world. You can follow his musings online at **@brandwithdrew**.

MERAKI HOUSE

P U B L I S H I N G

Publishing with Soul, Creativity & Love

Meraki House Publishing, founded in 2015 has established its brand as an independent virtual publishing house designed to suit your needs as the Author, delivering the highest quality design, writing and editorial, publishing and marketing services to ensure your success.

"Where your needs as an Author have become ours as an independent Publishing House."

WWW.MERAKIHOUSE.COM

In partnership with
www.designisreborn.com

Marnie Kay, Founder & CEO
marniekay.com